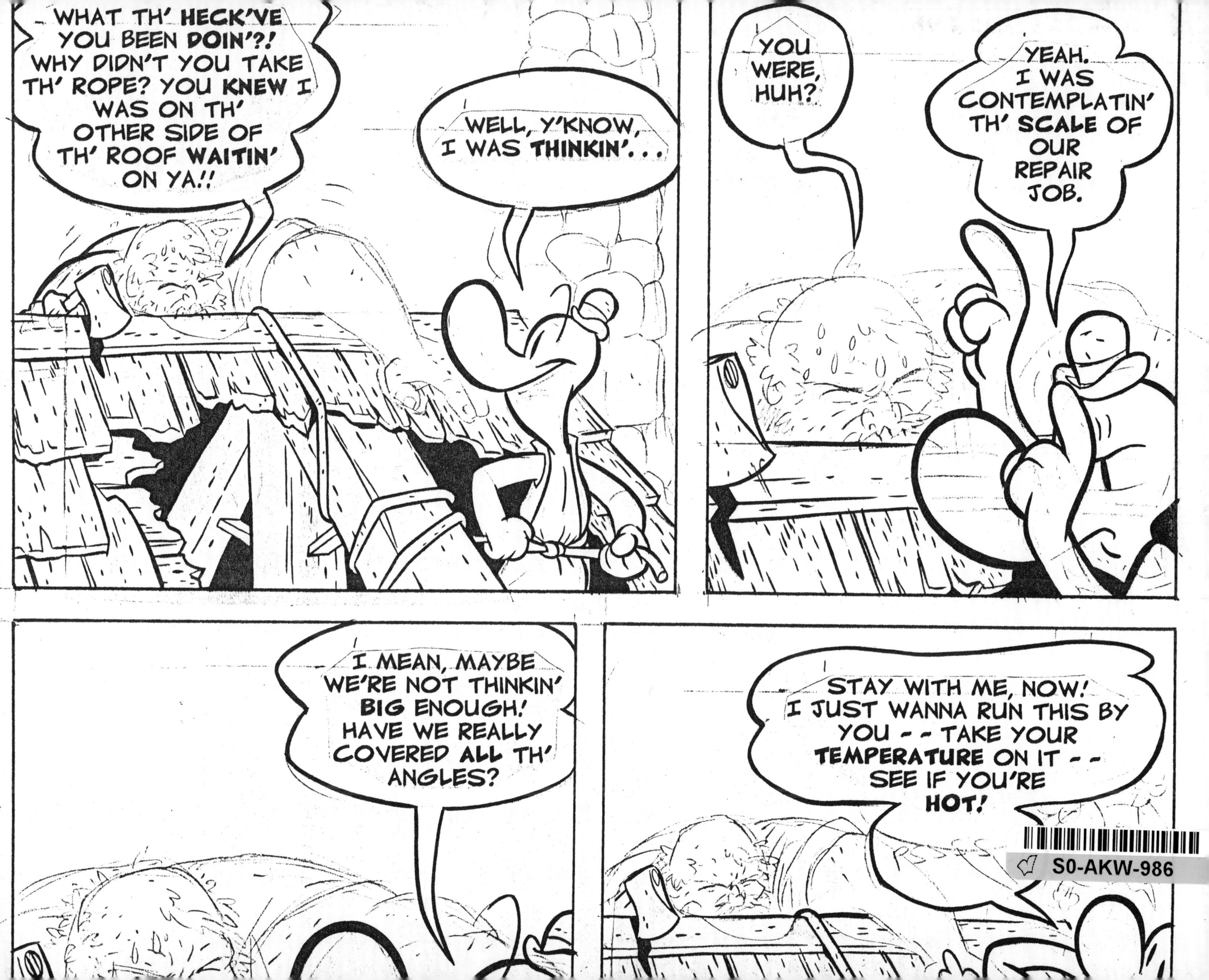
WHAT TH' HECK'VE YOU BEEN DOIN'?! WHY DIDN'T YOU TAKE TH' ROPE? YOU KNEW I WAS ON TH' OTHER SIDE OF TH' ROOF WAITIN' ON YA!!
WELL, Y'KNOW, I WAS THINKIN'. . .
YOU WERE, HUH?
YEAH. I WAS CONTEMPLATIN' TH' SCALE OF OUR REPAIR JOB.
I MEAN, MAYBE WE'RE NOT THINKIN' BIG ENOUGH! HAVE WE REALLY COVERED ALL TH' ANGLES?
STAY WITH ME, NOW! I JUST WANNA RUN THIS BY YOU -- TAKE YOUR TEMPERATURE ON IT -- SEE IF YOU'RE HOT!

Jeff Smith
Bone and Beyond

# Jeff Smith: Bone and Beyond

Lucy Shelton Caswell and David Filipi

Wexner Center for the Arts
The Ohio State University
Columbus, Ohio
2008

Published in association with

**Jeff Smith**
**Bone and Beyond**

Organized by
Wexner Center for the Arts
Cartoon Research Library
The Ohio State University

May 10–August 3, 2008

*Jeff Smith: Bone and Beyond*
received major support from
Scholastic, Inc.

**◪ SCHOLASTIC**

All Wexner Center exhibitions
receive support from the
Corporate Annual Fund of the
Wexner Center Foundation and
Wexner Center members.

PREFERRED AIRLINE
American Airlines/American Eagle

ACCOMMODATIONS
The Blackwell Inn

Project team

CURATORS
Lucy Shelton Caswell and
David Filipi

CURATORIAL ASSISTANT
Nancy Schindele

EXHIBITIONS MANAGER
Jill Davis

HEAD REGISTRAR
Megan Cavanaugh

PREPARATOR
Will Fugman

CARTOON RESEARCH LIBRARY LIAISONS
Jenny Robb
Susan Liberator
Marilyn Scott
Jillian Carney
Colin McDonald

GRAPHIC DESIGNER
M. Christopher Jones

EDITOR
Ann Bremner

Published by
Wexner Center for the Arts
The Ohio State University
1871 North High Street
Columbus, Ohio 43210-1393
USA
Tel:     +(614) 292-0330
Fax:    +(614) 292-3369
www.wexarts.org

Distributed by
D.A.P. Distributed Art
Publishers, Inc.
155 Sixth Avenue, 2nd Floor
New York, New York 10013
USA
Tel:     +(212) 627-1999
          +(800) 338-2665
Fax:    +(212) 627-9484
www.artbook.com

© 2008 The Ohio State University,
Wexner Center for the Arts.
All rights reserved.

ISBN: 978-1-881390-46-6

Library of Congress Control Number:
2008925254

Printed by Century Graphics,
Columbus, Ohio.
Text paper is Scheufelen
PhoeniXmotion Xenon 115# Text.
Endleaf paper is Mohawk Navajo
Brilliant White 100# Text.
Typefaces are Fedra Sans Display,
Glypha, and Warnock Pro.

Cover images

FRONT
*Bone* 40, cover, color, 2001
Colored by Elizabeth Lewis
Courtesy of Jeff Smith, Cartoon Books
This is the only wraparound cover in the series.

BACK
*Bone* 20, cover, color, 1995
Ink, airbrush, and colored pencils;
airbrush by David Reed
17 x 11⅝ in.

Endleaf images

*Bone* 12, p. 2 (details), 1994
(*Bone: The Complete Cartoon Epic
in One Volume*, p. 260, details)
These details show different stages of the drawing process.

**A Note on the Images**

Images are original art by Jeff Smith unless otherwise indicated. *Bone* images are indentified by issue number, page number, and where applicable, by the corresponding page number in *Bone: The Complete Cartoon Epic in One Volume* (Columbus, Ohio: Cartoon Books, 2004). © 1991–2008 by Jeff Smith.

Images by other artists are also original art, except for those by Carl Barks. Additional credits appear with the images.

All images are from the collection of The Ohio State University Cartoon Research Library, unless another source is acknowledged. Works from *Bone* are from the library's Jeff Smith Deposit Collection.

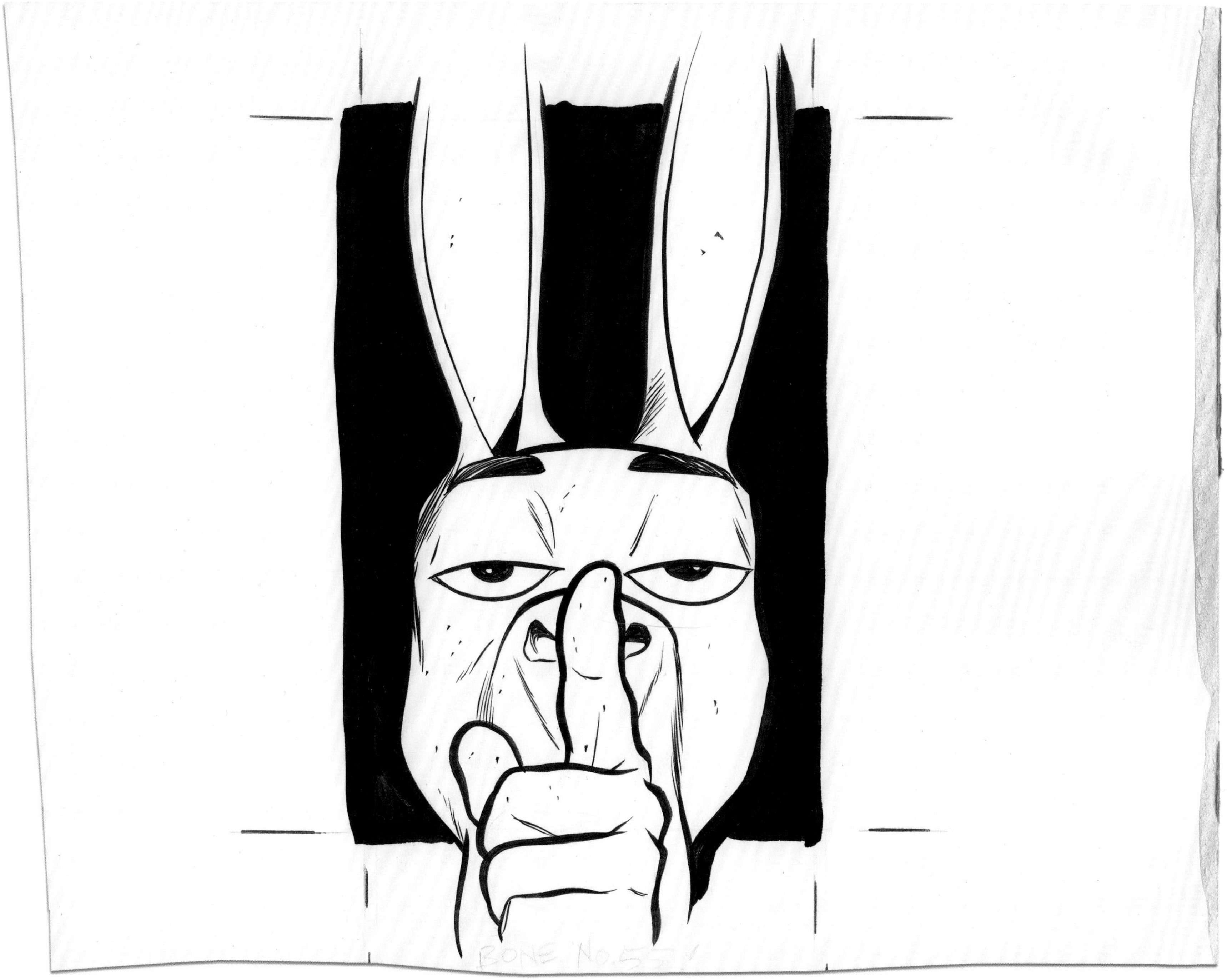
BONE No.55

*Bone* 55, cover, black and white, 2004
Ink and blue pencil on paper
$8\frac{7}{8}$ x $6\frac{15}{16}$ in.

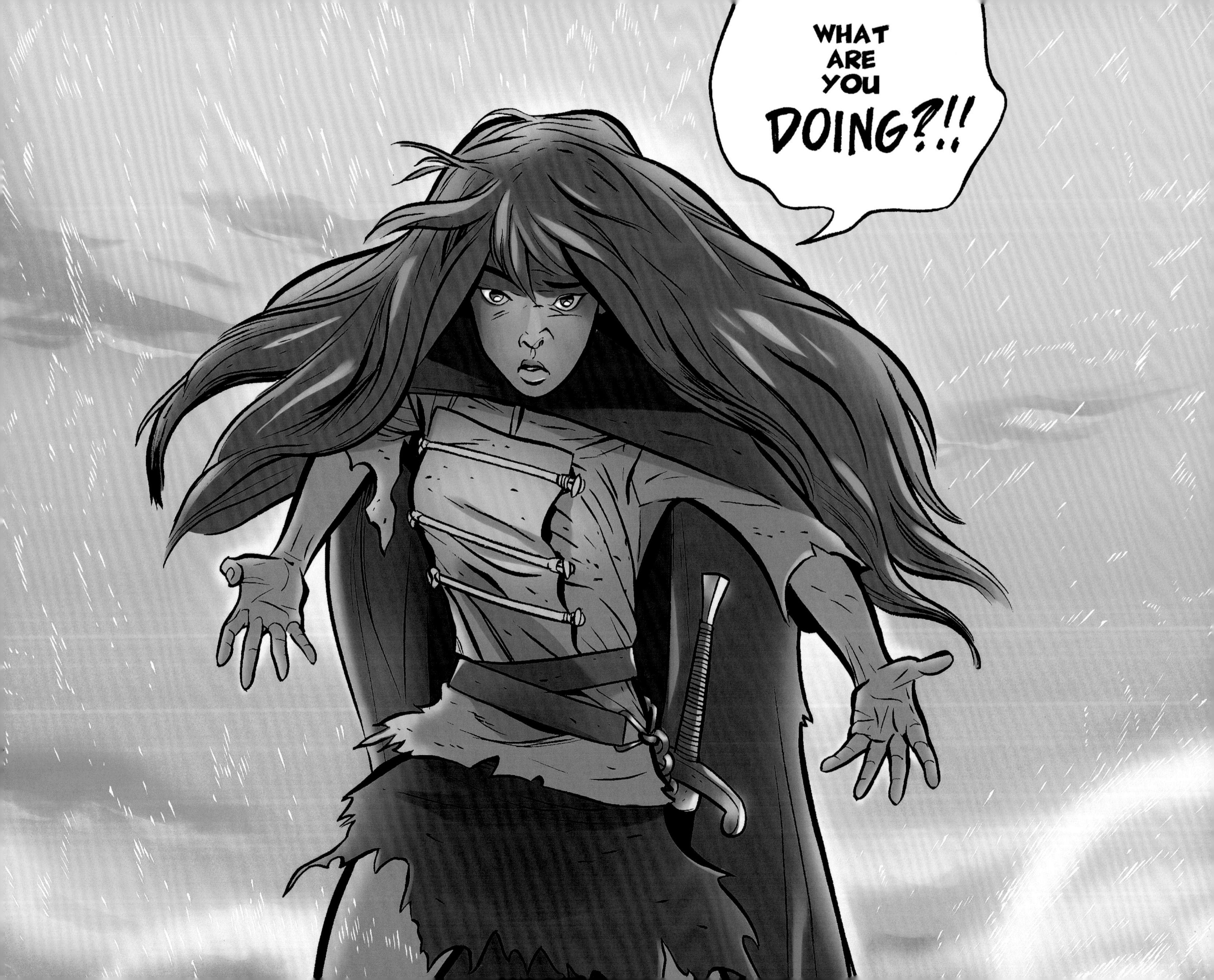
WHAT ARE YOU DOING?!!

# Foreword

Jeff Smith's *Bone* is a certified international phenomenon—an independent, self-published comic book series that's earned critical acclaim and commercial success, been translated into sixteen languages, and is now reaching even more readers in a nine-volume full-color edition published by Scholastic, the same company that brought Harry Potter to America. With *Bone and Beyond*, Smith receives his first solo exhibition in a museum setting, where his work will surely delight his many fans and introduce new viewers to his appealing characters and their adventures.

To organize and mount this exhibition, the Wexner Center has joined forces with Ohio State's Cartoon Research Library, our valued colleagues and close neighbors on the university's campus. (Indeed the Cartoon Research Library is housed in an underground extension of the Wexner Center building, though it is administratively separate as part of the university's library system.) We've worked together in the past on lectures and film screenings, but this exhibition is certainly our most extensive collaboration to date.

Our partnership in this instance was quite serendipitous. Wexner Center Film Curator Dave Filipi found himself visiting the Cartoon Research Library's relatively small exhibition space, and he inquired of Lucy Shelton Caswell, professor and curator of the Cartoon Research Library, whether there had ever been a project that she eagerly wished to pursue but couldn't because of limited gallery space. Her immediate response was "yes, Jeff Smith," and thus began a formidable collaboration. Caswell, of course, brings her breadth of knowledge and depth of insights into the history and current practices of cartoons, comics, and related arts. Filipi, who has long championed the prominent inclusion of animation in the center's screening schedule, brings a keen and lifelong engagement with cartoons and comics, whether in still or moving pictures. There couldn't have been a better partnership for Filipi's first foray into exhibition making.

As the title *Bone and Beyond* suggests, the exhibition's primary focus is on Smith's original drawings for his epic. The show features numerous original black and white pages from *Bone* and a smaller selection of full-color *Bone* covers. We're pleased to also exhibit selections from two subsequent projects:

Smith's recent *Shazam* series (featuring the early life of Captain Marvel) for DC Comics and *Rasl*, a story about a time-travelling art thief. From this later work, it is clear that Smith's art has continued to develop and grow, even as his reputation for *Bone* has continued to soar.

As you'll note from the extensive conversation captured in this volume, Jeff Smith is inspired and engaged by the works of his artistic forebears in cartoons and comics, a fascination—I should add—that in no way undercuts the independence and originality of his own creations. We're delighted that in this exhibition Smith's drawings share the gallery with examples from so many of the comics he cites as influences, among them Walt Kelly's *Pogo*, Will Eisner's *The Spirit*, George Herriman's *Krazy Kat*, Charles Schulz's *Peanuts*, Garry Trudeau's *Doonesbury*, Carl Barks's *Uncle Scrooge*, and E. C. Segar's *Thimble Theatre*. As it turns out, Smith first met Caswell and discovered the Cartoon Research Library while still an undergraduate student at Ohio State, and both were clearly valuable resources to him as he explored the varied heritage of his chosen medium. The majority of the exhibited works by these other artists are drawn from the collection of the Cartoon Research Library, which merits our utmost gratitude in that regard.

Jeff Smith's enthusiastic collaboration with the co-curators and with numerous staff members from throughout the Wexner Center has been truly remarkable, and I thank him for so graciously sharing his work, his time, and his virtually boundless energy with all of us and with our audience. I also express my enormous gratitude to both Lucy Shelton Caswell and David Filipi for so avidly embracing this project in the midst of already considerable workloads. Together they have crafted a splendid pageant of Smith's work and influences. I trust the rewards of contemplating the exhibition in the gallery and perusing the pages of this handsome catalogue in some measure repay their unstinting investment in this endeavor.

In addition, I gratefully acknowledge Scholastic for a most generous gift in support of the exhibition. It's gratifying to know that *Bone*'s distinguished publisher is willing to foster the kind of curatorial and critical inquiry represented by this project. American Airlines / American Eagle and the Blackwell

*Bone* 27, p. 12, 1997
(*Bone: The Complete Cartoon Epic in One Volume*, p. 596)
Image colored by Steve Hamaker for *Bone* book 4 in the Scholastic edition

hotel and conference center have also contributed generously to *Jeff Smith: Bone and Beyond* as well as two concurrent exhibitions at the Wexner Center.

The acknowledgments at the back of this volume express the curators' appreciation to those who have participated most actively in realizing this exhibition and accompanying catalogue. I am honored to join them in that expression of gratitude, just as I know they join me in recognizing the Wexner Center's Board, staff, and volunteers for their myriad contributions to this project, as to all our endeavors.

Sherri Geldin
Director
Wexner Center for the Arts

THOSE RAT CREATURES WOULD HAVE TO BE PRETTY STUPID TO FOLLOW ME ON TO THIS FRAIL, LITTLE BRANCH!
STUPID, STUPID RAT CREATURES!!

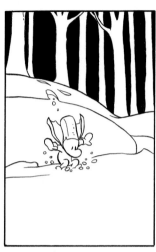

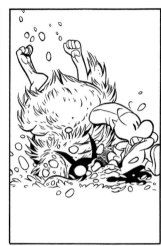

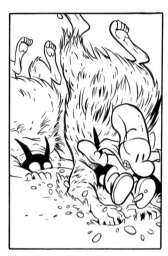

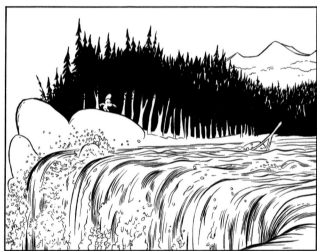

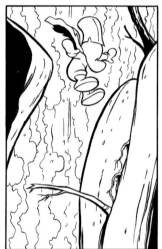

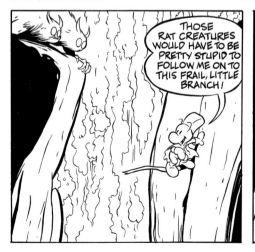

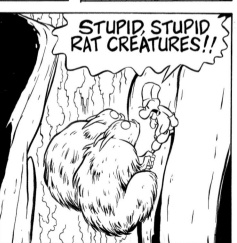

# Introduction

This is not a retrospective. Instead it is a celebration of the completion of a monumental task—the publication of more than 1300 pages of graphic narrative—and an overview of Jeff Smith's work at the height of his creative powers. Cartoonists are both writers and artists. Some, like Jeff Smith, are storytellers. Early in the *Bone* epic, he takes stock characters—everyman, the con artist, and the simpleton—and makes them his own. As readers we accept the reality (and humanity) of the doughy Bone cousins, and we care about what happens to them. The fact that their story was both carefully written and beautifully drawn makes it a masterwork. Smith followed *Bone* with a four–comic book series featuring Captain Marvel. His take on Billy Batson as a child was informed by his mother's belief in the power of Shazam. Where *Rasl*, his latest work, will take us is yet to unfold.

The art in this exhibition was not created for display in a gallery. It was intended to be read, with each reader personally holding and responding to the creator's page. Most gallery shows feature pictures without words. Cartoons by definition include both words and pictures in that mysterious interconnected synergy where meaning is incomplete until both are read. Curating an exhibition of such work creates challenges. Should a gallery exhibition of sequential graphic narrative attempt to replicate the intimate experience of reading a book? Is it possible to capture the scope, depth, and breadth of the *Bone* narrative with the number of works that a reasonable gallery visitor might be expected to read during a visit? How can samples of an extended story be made accessible to those unfamiliar with the tale? How can Smith's artistic influences be integrated into the show in such a way that visitors can understand how one generation stands on the shoulders of another to reach greatness without imitating what has gone before?

Dave Filipi, co-curator of this exhibition, and I began by rereading all 1300+ pages of *Bone* with sticky notes in hand. After "must include" and "maybe" pages were reviewed, we then talked with Smith, who had his own list of "musts." There were no disagreements. The problem was limited space and the reality of visitor fatigue after reading page after page while standing in a gallery. To narrow the field, we concentrated on pages that were exemplars of the highpoints of Smith's work such as his use of animation techniques, slapstick, pantomime, and the slight gesture.

Early on we decided to include a complete *Bone* story. Elsewhere in this volume, Smith describes issue sixteen of *Bone* (reproduced on pages 35 to 61) in which he created a twenty-page story that would take readers approximately twenty minutes to read. Because much of issue sixteen is wordless, it was the ideal example for the exhibit. The interplay of thunder and lightning is the key to the passage of time in this episode—and Smith's mastery of both pacing and narrative is remarkable.

Throughout his career Smith has gladly acknowledged those cartoonists who influenced him. That he cites Charles Schulz, Walt Kelly, E. C. Segar, Carl Barks, George Herriman, Will Eisner, and Garry Trudeau as significant is not surprising since their importance would be acknowledged by most thoughtful cartoonists of Smith's generation. What is unusual, however, is the way it is possible to relate these cartoonists' work to Smith's very directly. For that reason, the examples of their work are integrated with that of Smith in the exhibition instead of being relegated to a separate section.

One of the effects of the Wexner Center for the Arts' focus on contemporary art is that curators frequently work with living artists. This was a particular advantage in the case of this exhibition. The insights provided by Jeff Smith were key to shaping the exhibit. The body of work from which to choose was so large, thanks to Smith's practice of retaining his original art, that choosing works would have been daunting had we not been able to talk with him. He and his partner, Vijaya Iyer, were patient to meet with us repeatedly to talk about the fine points of the exhibition—and the exhibition is much richer for this.

The collected edition of *Bone* recently went into its tenth printing, meaning that more than 100,000 copies are in print. It is a privilege to share Smith's original artwork in a gallery setting for his readers to enjoy and to introduce it to visitors who might be unfamiliar with it.

Lucy Shelton Caswell
Professor and Curator
Cartoon Research Library

*Bone* 2, p. 9, 1991
(*Bone: The Complete Cartoon Epic in One Volume*, p. 47)
Ink and blue pencil on paper
17 x 14 in.

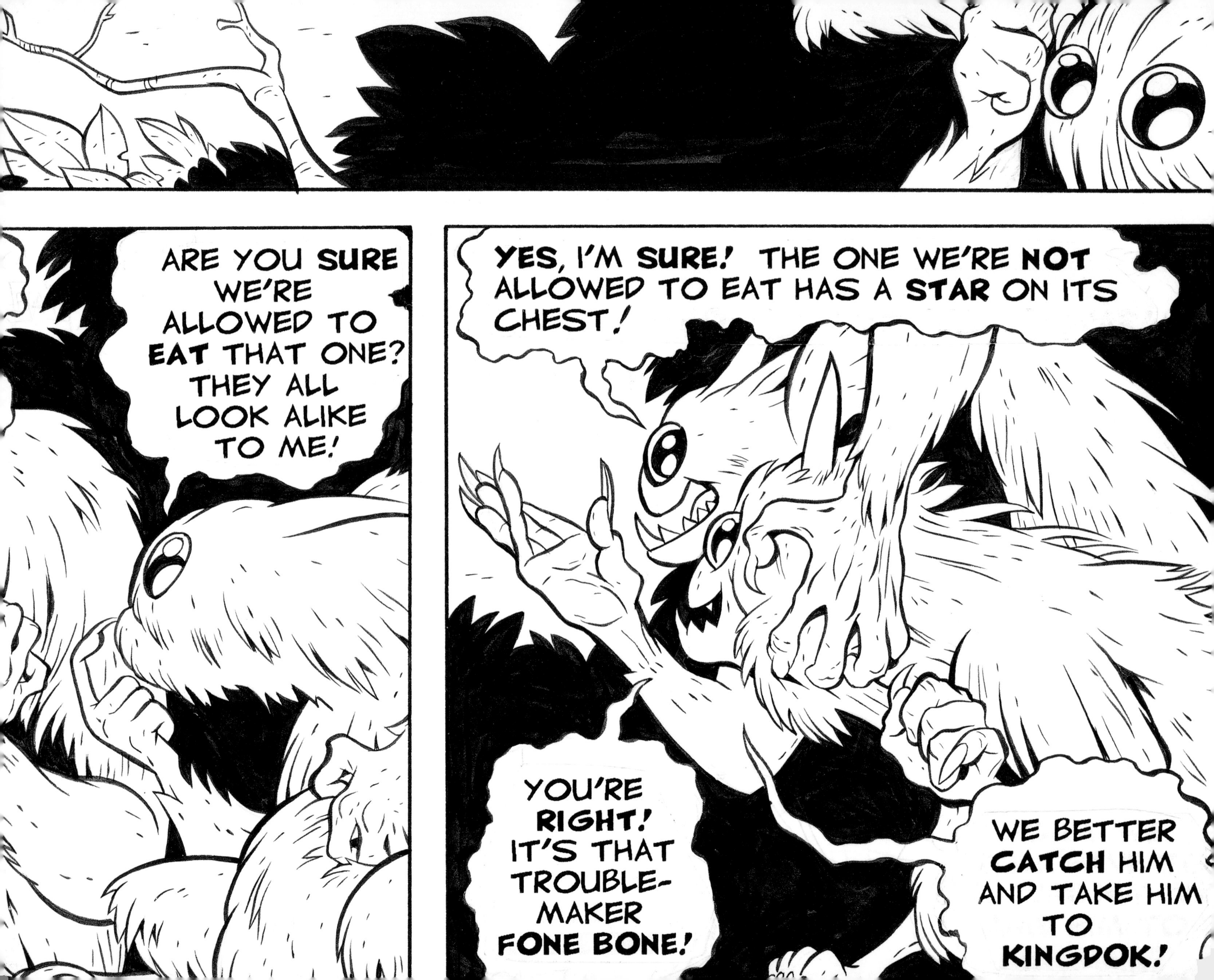
ARE YOU SURE WE'RE ALLOWED TO EAT THAT ONE? THEY ALL LOOK ALIKE TO ME!
YES, I'M SURE! THE ONE WE'RE NOT ALLOWED TO EAT HAS A STAR ON ITS CHEST!
YOU'RE RIGHT! IT'S THAT TROUBLE-MAKER FONE BONE!
WE BETTER CATCH HIM AND TAKE HIM TO KINGDOK!

# A Conversation with Jeff Smith

Lucy Shelton Caswell and David Filipi

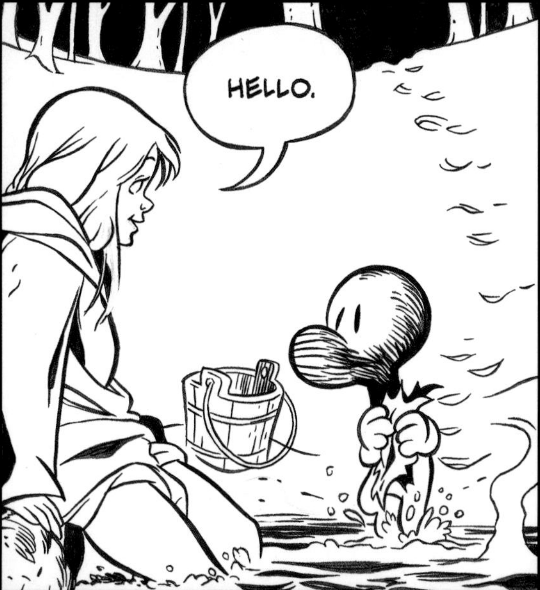
HELLO.

"PEANUTS"
4-9
Tm. Reg. U. S. Pat Off.—All rights reserved Copr. 1955 by United Feature Syndicate, Inc.
SCHULZ

IS THAT A "WOTT" ON HER CHEEK ?
NO, IT'S NOT A WART - IT'S A "BEAUTY SPOT"
© 1934, King Features Syndicate, Inc., Great Britain rights reserved.
ALL THE BEST "BEAUX" AND "BELLES" WEAR THEM
ME, TOO, WILL BE A "BO" AN' A "BELL".
GLUE
WELL - - ?
WELL WHAT ?
5-29
HERRIMAN

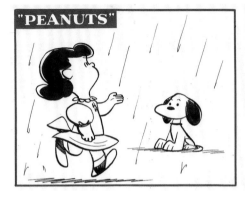

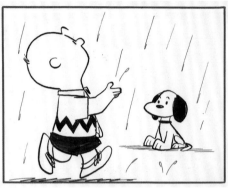

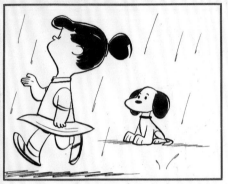

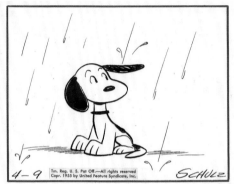

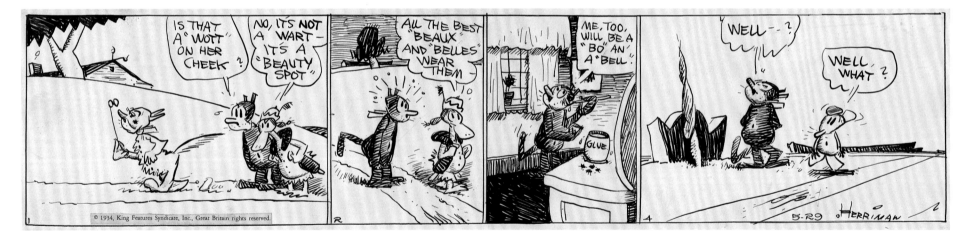

**DF — Can you remember when you were first exposed to the work of some of the people you have cited as influences, who are included in the show?**

JS — *Peanuts* was almost unavoidable. Everybody read *Peanuts*, especially in the 1960s, because it was in the Sunday paper. But I actually remember the first time *Peanuts* got under my skin was when my mom bought me a little paperback collection, like one of those little 25-cent paperbacks. It was mostly silent. It was a collection of Snoopy strips. There wasn't a lot of talking so I could almost read it. This would have been when I was about four—so before I was even able to read. And I remember that what actually got me to learn to read was trying to figure out what was happening with Snoopy and Charlie Brown in these little book collections, because I didn't have my parents there reading to me like I did with the Sunday paper. I was by myself with this book, and I just had to figure out what Charlie Brown and Snoopy were doing.

**DF — It is interesting that you mentioned Charles Schulz first because one can assume that you would be exposed to Charlie Brown and *Peanuts* at an early age. But how does someone your age get exposed to E. C. Segar, George Herriman, and people like that? It is unlikely you would just walk into a store and find reprints.**

JS — Some of the influences are the kind that you see at a very early age and some come almost by osmosis—they get into you. It's not like I studied Schulz. He informed my sense of humor in the way I drew faces and things like that. Then there are the influences that you get later on. When I was going to Ohio State, I met Lucy and she had the early incarnation of the Cartoon Research Library. That was the first time I saw some real serious collections of old, classic, golden age newspaper strips. In the library I found a book of the old Segar *Thimble Theatres* that reprinted the first year of the strip, and it blew me away. At that time I was already doing *Thorn*, which was basically an early version of *Bone*, in the Ohio State *Lantern*, but it was still unformed, a beginning version. Segar changed the texture of the strip: I picked up his more abrupt sense of humor and pacing, and that began to work its way into the *Thorn* strip from that point on.

**DF — When you say the "abrupt" pacing, what do you mean?**

JS — His jokes were kind of coarse—and fast. When you make a comic you always have to be aware of any two given panels working together. What happens to the subject from one panel to the next defines the amount of time that takes place between the two panels. So in a Segar comic, if Popeye's in jail, when he wants to get out of jail, he just tears the bars down. Segar wouldn't waste any panels of *Popeye* pulling on the bars. One second he's standing there; the next second the bars are flying. That's what I meant by abruptness. He intuitively knew how to pace the drawings in the panels. I call it "abrupt" because it catches you off guard—it's a bit of surprise—and it's a large part of his sense of humor. I started using that in the strips a lot, too. I discovered Herriman around the same time, probably in comic book stores. In comic book stores, I began to see a more layered world of comics, where you had the undergrounds, you had alternatives, you had *Superman*, and you had collections being put out by, say, Kitchen Sink, of *Krazy Kat*. And they were really beautiful reproductions. There's real care being put into these books. And there's another kind of...I won't use the same word, it's not abrupt...

Charles M. Schulz
*Peanuts*, April 9, 1955
Ink on paper
6 x 28½ in.


George Herriman
*Krazy Kat*, May 29, 1934
Ink on paper
5¼ x 21 in.

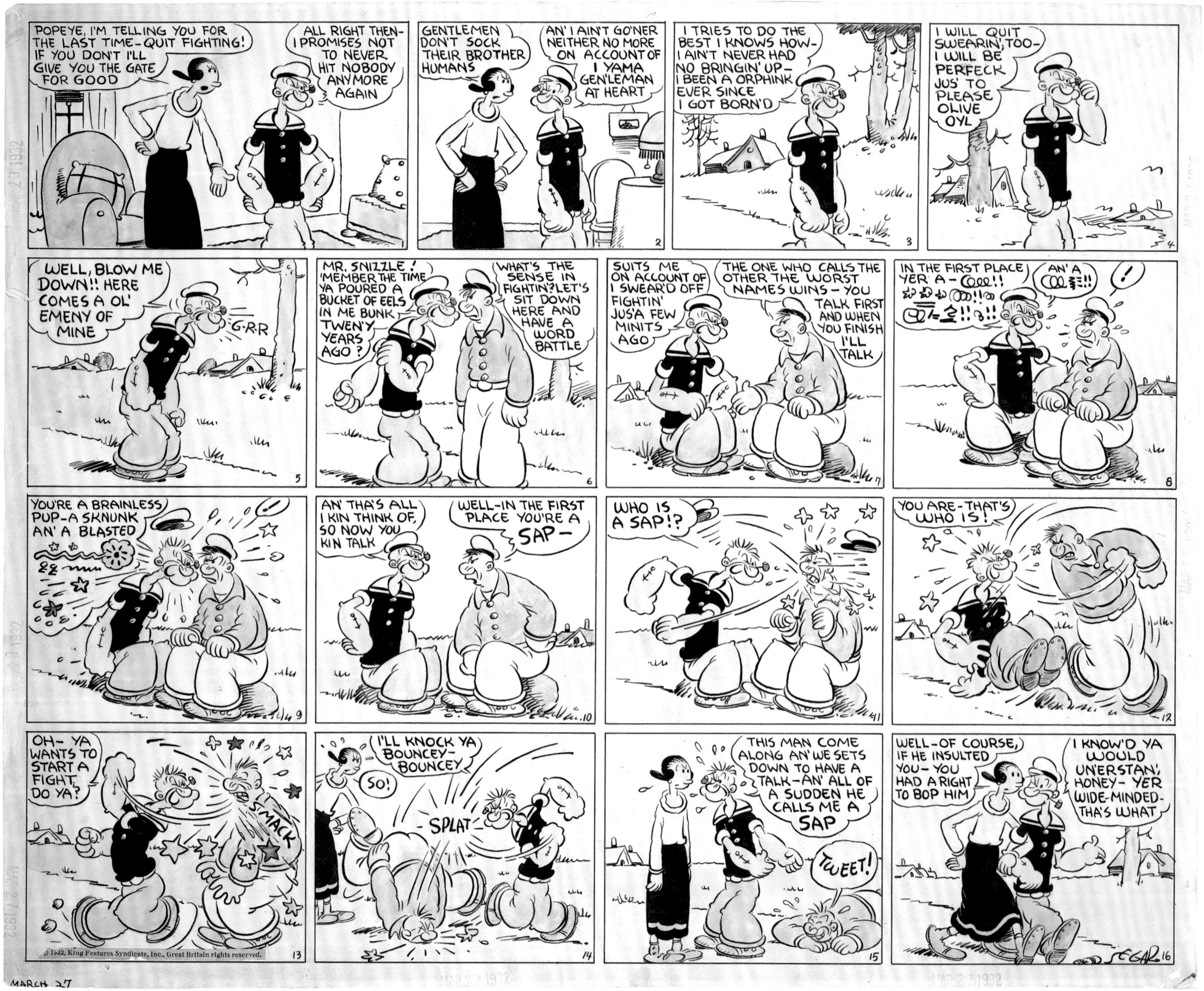
POPEYE, I'M TELLING YOU FOR THE LAST TIME-QUIT FIGHTING! IF YOU DON'T I'LL GIVE YOU THE GATE FOR GOOD
ALL RIGHT THEN- I PROMISES NOT TO NEVER HIT NOBODY ANYMORE AGAIN
GENTLEMEN DON'T SOCK THEIR BROTHER HUMANS
AN' I AIN'T GO'NER NEITHER NO MORE ON ACCOUNT OF I YAMA GEN'LEMAN AT HEART
I TRIES TO DO THE BEST I KNOWS HOW- I AIN'T NEVER HAD NO BRINGIN' UP- I BEEN A ORPHINK EVER SINCE I GOT BORN'D
I WILL QUIT SWEARIN', TOO- I WILL BE PERFECK JUS' TO PLEASE OLIVE OYL
WELL, BLOW ME DOWN!! HERE COMES A OL' EMENY OF MINE
G-R-R
MR. SNIZZLE! 'MEMBER THE TIME YA POURED A BUCKET OF EELS IN ME BUNK TWEN'Y YEARS AGO?
WHAT'S THE SENSE IN FIGHTIN'? LET'S SIT DOWN HERE AND HAVE A WORD BATTLE
SUITS ME ON ACCOUNT OF I SWEAR'D OFF FIGHTIN' JUS'A FEW MINITS AGO
THE ONE WHO CALLS THE OTHER THE WORST NAMES WINS- YOU TALK FIRST AND WHEN YOU FINISH I'LL TALK
IN THE FIRST PLACE YER A-
AN' A
!
YOU'RE A BRAINLESS PUP-A SKNUNK AN' A BLASTED
AN' THA'S ALL I KIN THINK OF, SO NOW YOU KIN TALK
WELL-IN THE FIRST PLACE YOU'RE A SAP-
WHO IS A SAP!?
YOU ARE-THAT'S WHO IS!
OH- YA WANTS TO START A FIGHT, DO YA?
SMACK
© 1932, King Features Syndicate, Inc., Great Britain rights reserved.
I'LL KNOCK YA BOUNCEY-BOUNCEY
SO!
SPLAT
THIS MAN COME ALONG AN' WE SETS DOWN TO HAVE A TALK-AN' ALL OF A SUDDEN HE CALLS ME A SAP
TWEET!
WELL-OF COURSE, IF HE INSULTED YOU- YOU HAD A RIGHT TO BOP HIM
I KNOW'D YA WOULD UN'ERSTAN', HONEY- YER WIDE-MINDED- THA'S WHAT
SEGAR
MARCH 27

but there's an edginess to Herriman's work, a looseness. Instead of saying "abrupt," I'll say it's more immediate. It feels like there's a stage of refinement missing in between Herriman and the reader that just feels more immediate.

**LSC—I want to go back to *Peanuts* and ask what was it that grabbed you about that comic strip?**

JS—The fact that the characters were thinking. Portraying the interior lives of these kids was so unprecedented at the time. I probably didn't think in those terms when I was five or six, but I still knew it, because you could watch cartoons on TV, you could see Bugs Bunny, you could see Heckle and Jeckle—these are all really good cartoons, but nobody talked about the troubling interior life the way Schulz did, and did so perfectly. When Charlie Brown made a fool of himself, or was embarrassed by the other kids, or he said his stomach hurt, you could see on his face that his stomach hurt. With two dots, and a squiggly line for a mouth, he showed you what Charlie Brown felt, and that is remarkable. He has such a wide range of characters—from Snoopy to Lucy and Linus and Schroeder—he just covered such a wide range of human emotion. Again, I didn't think about that when I was a kid—probably nobody really does—but it reaches you. And so that's why I think it works so well.

**DF—You mentioned that early on you were more influenced by strips or perhaps "influenced" is not the right word at that time in your life, but you were more exposed to comic strips than to comic books. It's interesting that a lot of your influences in the show are strip artists, yet *Bone* is not a strip work. It's a longer-form work. How did that happen? Why were you not more influenced by longer-form artists?**

PEANUTS
I GUESS ONE OF THE THINGS WE ALL HAVE TO LEARN IS TO LIVE JUST ONE DAY AT A TIME..
Tm. Reg. U. S. Pat. Off.—All rights reserved Copr. 1958 by United Feature Syndicate, Inc.
I DO BETTER THAN THAT... I LIVE JUST ONE SECOND AT A TIME.. THERE! THAT WAS A GOOD ONE!
HERE COMES ANOTHER ONE... THERE! I LIVED PRETTY GOOD DURING THAT ONE... THERE! OH, THAT WAS A HAPPY SECOND..
6-4
THERE! OH, I WAS REAL GOOD DURING THAT ONE.. HERE COMES ANOTHER ONE..
I CAN'T STAND IT!
SCHULZ

E. C. Segar
*Thimble Theatre*, 1932
Pen and ink on illustration board
17 x 21⅝ in.
International Museum of Cartoon Art


Charles M. Schulz
*Peanuts*, June 4, 1958
Ink on paper
2 panels, 6 x 13¾ in. each

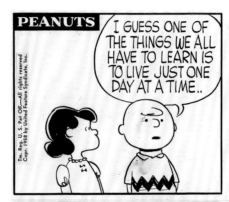

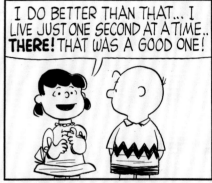

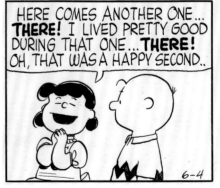

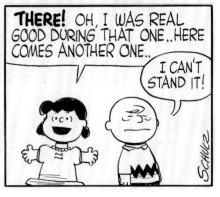

JS——Well, the short answer is that there weren't too many longer-form artists back then.

DF——**I meant working with an issue of a comic book as opposed to a strip.**

JS——I think it's because the two art forms have such different working methods. The comic strip started off as sort of an auteur medium where you had a single artist who wrote it and drew the strip. The comic books from the beginning were a very commercial enterprise where you had an editor or a company that was creating characters for sale, and they would hire someone to write it and hire somebody else to pencil it. It was a real factory process creating that kind of a book. They had somebody doing the lettering, somebody doing the inking. There was some of that in comic strips, but not to the same extent. I was just more drawn to the auteur work. That's why when I found the comic book stores, and I discovered the auteur work in the independent comic books, that's when I began a shift toward them. Also, I submitted my comic strip to every syndicate that existed, and they all turned me down. So I didn't have any choice.

LSC——**You did have a choice. You could have done it and adapted it the way some of them suggested.**

JS——That's very true. And that's why when I discovered a place that I felt was a more fertile ground for my type of comics—comic books—I didn't hesitate to move over in that direction. So I actually don't see that much of a disconnect between the kind of influences that we're including in the show like Herriman and Schulz and comic books, because it's that single-author-ness that is the connection between those strips and my work. And there are certainly other comic book artists that fit that category now.

LSC——**You came to know what your direction was as a very young person. I think that's rather unusual.**

JS——It sounds more unusual than it seems, I think, because even though I loved comics and I wanted to do them, I didn't set out to be a cartoonist or anything like that from the get-go. I didn't say, "I know what I'm going to do and I'm going to do it," like Mozart writing symphonies and never looking back. I went through high school, and I did not know what I was going to do for a living. I had no idea. I didn't know if I was going to get into animation and go and try and get a job at Disney. The fact that I ended up, once I got into college, actually really trying to do what I wanted to do as a little kid, kind of brought the circle back around. I'm not trying to say I knew I was going to be a cartoonist the whole way through.

LSC——**You did a sort of prototype of the story that became *Bone* as an undergraduate and had the arc of the story already percolating in your mind.**

JS——Right. Interestingly, I didn't. When I started the comic strip in college, I was very jazzed by certain strips, like *Doonesbury*, which had a lightly continuing storyline that would go on for very long periods, and of course my childhood loves of *Peanuts* and *Uncle Scrooge*. Then the last big, big influence on me before I started the comic was *Métal Hurlant*, *Heavy Metal*, Moebius and Enki Bilal, and all those guys doing kind of grown-up fantasy stories or mythological stories. So being able to mix those kinds of things together—*Doonesbury* and *Uncle Scrooge* and *Heavy Metal*—that was what I felt was the subject matter that would interest me, and I came up with the cast while drawing the comic strip. But it actually bugged me that I didn't have a story. I had these three Bone characters, and they all had personalities, and it seemed like there was a lot I could do with them. They were really fun to work with. And I had all these characters for them to work against—the dragons and the monsters and the humans that lived in the environment. But there was no point to it, and it kind of bugged me. Why don't these characters have some reason for being in this story? I started to understand that I was missing an underpinning. I was missing some depth. I wanted to find out what inspired George Lucas and what inspired Tolkien. And that's how I discovered Joseph Campbell, who was a big inspiration for Lucas to build his *Star Wars* stories on mythology. So from Lucas and Joseph Campbell, I started reading mythology starting with Greek mythology, but then discovering Indian mythologies. It was the same with Tolkien. Tolkien was all Celtic folktales and stuff, and I really got into that material. I began to understand that there are two directions for a story. There is the linear one that goes from beginning to middle and end, which I always wanted to do from the time I was a kid. But what builds that story? That's where you get into the symbolism and mythology…that's the art. And that gives it depth.

**DF** — **So you were consciously combining the art stories and the mythological works that you were reading at the same time? You were very conscious of that?**

JS — I was very conscious of it. My thought was if you're going to put this much work into something—because comics are a heck of a lot of work—it better be something you like to draw. And the two things that interested me were the *Heavy Metal*, adult fantasy type of comics, and *Pogo* and the Carl Barks's *Uncle Scrooge* material. I just thought you can put those two together, and I thought you would have something that would meld and be funny and entertaining. That's what I wanted to work in. And it wasn't until later that I began to feel that it needed more, that it needed a depth to it that I found in symbolism and mythology.

**DF** — **I think part of it, too, is getting older and getting more life experience.**

JS — Certainly. By the time I finished *Bone*, which was a thirteen-year process, I had begun to travel. As *Bone* got published in more and more languages, Vijaya and I were being invited to different countries. We would explore all of the cathedrals and the art we would see there, the culture there. Then my life experiences began to really impact *Bone*, which worked because the Bones were having the same experience in the story as they explored the valley and found new civilizations. So, yes, it does. I guess as you get older you are more interested in symbolism in art anyway.

**DF** — **It sounds like a natural progression where you created the characters and you created the world that you wanted them to inhabit, but you were frustrated because you wanted there to be more meaning in what you were working on. It seems natural to me that after being exposed to all different types of things in college that you would want to expand it.**

JS — I thought because *Bone* was a serialized story that took years to complete, I would get feedback and I would find that people would enjoy things that had some meat to them. People enjoy things that have meaning. It became one of the secret pleasures of making comics—doing this research, blocking out time in my work day to go online and just follow one myth through its many permutations around the world, or to plan a trip to Kathmandu and go spend time and say, "this is going to be an alleyway right here that is going to appear in *Bone*." I started to really, really enjoy doing the research—and then always felt like there was a lot of reward for doing it because I could tell people would be enthusiastic about the results.

**DF—A minute ago you mentioned Carl Barks, and a number of people have noted the similarities between *Bone* and Barks's *Uncle Scrooge* stories. Do you remember the effect these stories had on you?**

JS—I remember there was nothing else like them. In those days, artists who worked on Disney comics were anonymous, but you could tell when Barks did a story. His art was so good. The line work on the characters was fine and detailed and the backgrounds were realistic. His stories were little gems. But it was the comics work itself that really grabbed me. His compositions and the positions of the characters within the frames as they transitioned from one panel to the next are kinetic. How far they had moved conveyed action, movement, and life. Those shirt-wearing ducks were real!

**LSC—Can you talk a little bit about Will Eisner?**

JS—Yes, I sure can. I first met him at Ohio State when he came to do a talk. I brought with me the first Will Eisner comic I encountered. And that's probably a better place to start. I found this reprint of his stuff. It was black and white—like an oversized magazine—in the early 1970s. So I was still a kid. I was probably ten or eleven, and I just was really knocked out by his artwork. His line style was filled with those really graceful thicks and thins—the same kind of

Philadelphia, June 12, 1949
PAGE 9
FUN BOOK—The Spirit
I HEADED BACK UP THE WINDING ROAD... THE WIND WAS STRONG AND A GENTLE RAIN BEGAN TO FALL... BUT THIS WAS NOTHING TO THE STORM RAGING WITHIN ME...
KURT WANTED THAT BRIEF CASE PRETTY BADLY... PERHAPS BADLY ENOUGH TO KILL FOR IT!
AS I REACHED THE PORTICO, I HEARD LOUD SHOUTING...
SATIN...YOU FOOL...YOU BUMBLING FOOL... WHY DID YOU BRING HIM?
KURT.. PLEASE.. NOT SO LOUD..
I WAS CERTAIN TO BE ACQUITTED!! ...NOW THAT MASKED MEDDLER WILL RUIN EVERYTHING... GOOD NIGHT!
..BETTER LOOK IN ON KURT...
THE DISPATCH CASE..SO IT WAS KURT'S MEN WHO JUMPED ME...
WELL,WELL... TESTIMONY BY SIR CLIVEDON... HMM... SEEMS THAT KURT VAN BRECK WAS USING HIS IMPORTING FIRM TO SMUGGLE CONTRABAND FROM SOUTH ASIA!
...IF THESE PAPERS GOT AROUND, THEY MIGHT PROVE DAMAGING... MIGHTN'T THEY, KURT?
YES, SPIRIT...AND A MAN MIGHT EVEN MURDER TO GET THESE PAPERS! GIVE THEM BACK TO ME!
KURT, HAVE YOU SEEN HILDIE? I CAN'T FIND HER ANYWHERE! AND STORM WARNINGS ARE BEING POSTED ALL OVER THE ISLAND... A HURRICANE IS RISING!
5

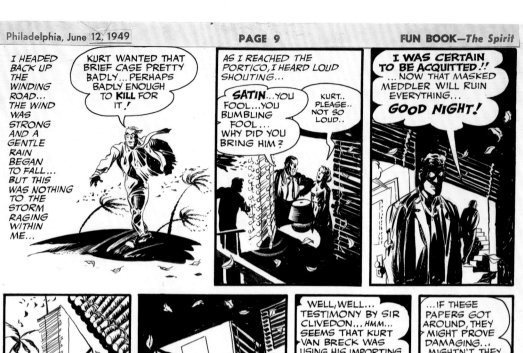

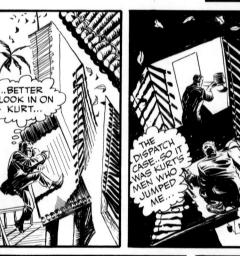

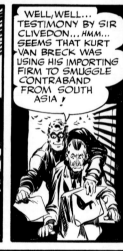

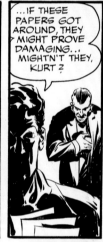

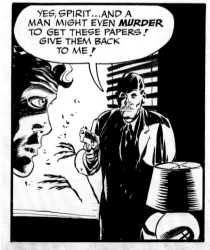

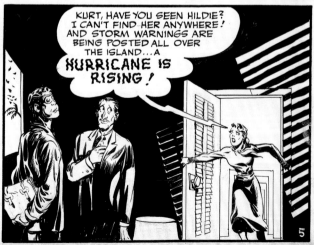

thing that appealed to me about Walt Kelly's line work. It was superb—extremely appealing. It was really dense and kind of dangerous at the same time. His stories were kind of superhero stories. The superhero guy had a suit on, but he still had a mask, which appealed to me as a kid. But the difference was that his stories had a *Twilight Zone* twist to them—an O'Henry type of twist. So they had the feeling of a short story, which gave them that heft or that weight that I said I felt was missing from my early comics. And I think it's missing from ninety-nine percent of all comics. But he had that in there. He had stories that were doing something, that were going somewhere. His characters were fully realized. And his work continued to have that kind of quality all they way up until he died.

Of course, in our industry, the comics industry, the major awards are named after him. While he was still alive, he would actually stand on stage during the Eisner Awards. He wasn't the presenter, but he would actually shake your hand and hand you your Eisner Award, when you went upstage. That was very exciting when I won my first Eisner Award. I felt he was genuinely happy for me. I actually got to know him quite well, and over the next ten years, which is how long he lived after I first met him, I would see him at different comic book shows, and I'd try to get some time with him in a bar or for a meal or something. He was one of those inspirational people. His mind never stopped thinking about comics and where they could go and what they could do, and what was the best potential for the reader. He was the guy who popularized the term "graphic novel" and was the first one to do one worthy of the name. I could go on and on about Will. I mean, as a human being he was just so warm and supportive, and he never missed an opportunity to pat you on the back and tell you to keep going.

DF—**Did you ever talk with him specifically about how he rewrote some of the rules: the layout of a page, the disregard for borders and panels and things like that?**

JS—I personally never actually consciously approached page layouts the way that how-to books tell you. I never found any of them to be very helpful, including Will's. However, there were many other elements of Will's how-to books that do express some kinds of movement—and the fact that he was one of the first to do it just gave it some weight. The one page layout I did use of Will's was what he calls the "meta-panel," which is where you have a large panel with insets. Usually it is used to convey some importance to the larger image. But I never spoke to him about that at all. What we would talk about would usually be industry matters. When I knew Will, the comic book industry was going through a very hard time. It was crashing, losing sales, stores were going out of business. This potential to take the graphic novel into the outer market was looming, but could we make it? Could we make the jump? We didn't know if it would happen, and we would talk a lot about that.

LSC—**In many ways, you and Will both marched to a different drummer.**

JS—I think Will recognized me as a fellow traveler, that's for sure. When you're talking about art, you can't have those kinds of concerns. To do something that doesn't fit into anything could make it great art, but not necessarily. But it makes some sense to abide by some rules. Like trying to get your comic book to try to fit into a certain category

Will Eisner
*The Spirit*, p.9, June 5, 1949
Ink on paper
22⅛ x 15 in.

so that people can sell it. Unlike a Matisse or a Picasso, these are popular art, mass art. You do want them to get out and get distributed. In that way comics have more in common with film than paintings. Because the original art is not the final product—the final product is the printed, mass-produced comic book. So the original page of art is sort of like the set or the script for a movie. The final product, of course, is the film. So what we're showing in this exhibit, I guess, would be like the equivalent of movie sets.

**LSC** — **Is there an anomaly then in doing gallery shows of original pages?**

JS — No, because there is an art in the comics. The art is kind of intangible, and the only people that really talked about it with any length or weight are Will Eisner and Scott McCloud. But there is an art to it. There is an art being communicated from the artist to the reader, and not in every comic, and not every idea is successful, but you have to approach it as art. That gets back to the breaking rules thing. Art just doesn't do well with rules. Art, in fact, thrives when the rules get broken. That's why people like me started trying to collect the books into these graphic novels to try to launch them out of our little tiny distribution system and get them into the other stores. I was part of a whole wave of artists that took up that call—just wouldn't do what we were supposed to do. But that's what is fun. That's what gets people interested. Now, many people are breaking the rules. More power to them. Break the rules, go on the Internet, and go forever. That was something Will Eisner would have said to me.

**DF** — **Just from looking at *Bone* there are definitely Joe Kubert influences. Could you talk about him?**

JS — What struck me about Kubert's work—in both of his most famous titles, *Sgt. Rock* and *Tarzan*—was his artwork. He had a completely individual line, like nobody else's—a big, fat, kind of greasy ink line that broke and blotched. And he didn't obsess about details, and in fact he would often leave out information. He might not even draw somebody's feet, but you always knew where the feet were. I came to appreciate that his artwork was in some ways better than the people who were drawing really perfect anatomically correct people. He engaged your imagination. I definitely brought that into my *Bone* work. Nothing I draw looks like Joe Kubert, but I was very conscious of how much information you had to impart because Joe knew exactly how much he needed to sell the idea completely. And I actually think that's more powerful—when you, the reader, fill in the feet. You do more than fill in the feet when you're doing that. You're filling in everything around the feet and behind them, and you make the world all the more real. The storytelling was really powerful. He could make an adventure story move. One minute he could have Tarzan standing there talking to someone, and you got Tarzan standing with his weight on one leg, like a real human would, instead of standing there with his hands on his hips like a superhero, and the next minute he's in the trees carrying a human being chased by gorillas, and it all looked completely real. It looked like that's really happening—and trees that are a hundred stories tall. It's just how he can make something impossible feel so plausible that you almost could feel the sunlight splashing by him and feel tree limbs under your feet. It's just amazing to me. Do you know how disappointed I was when I found out that trees in Africa weren't as tall as the Empire State Building?

DOONESBURY
by Garry Trudeau
© 1974 G. B. Trudeau
UNIVERSAL PRESS SYNDICATE
CLACKITY!
CLAK! CLACKITY! CLACK
3-19
TIME
The New Hedonism
CAMPUS '74
EXTRA! LATEST STUDENT MOOD!
Chicago Tri
on sale here
"SEX! SEX AND PEYOTE!" HE REPLIED.
I'M IN BIG TROUBLE..
GBTrudeau

Garry Trudeau
*Doonesbury*, March 16, 1974
Ink, benday, blue pencil on paper
6 x 16½ in.
International Museum of Cartoon Art


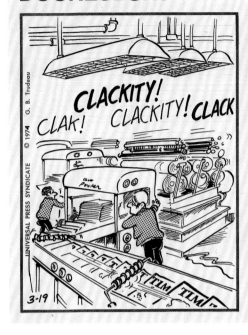

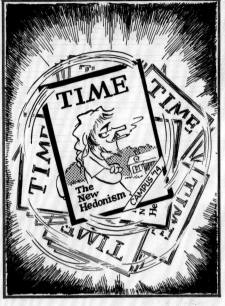

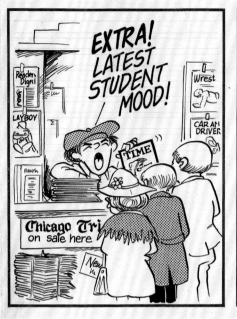

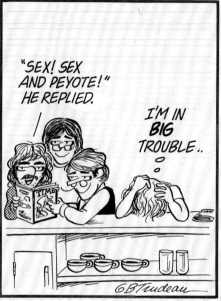

**DF — In a totally different vein, what about Garry Trudeau?**

JS — Well, Garry Trudeau stimulated my curiosity about politics and about the way politics work. When I say "politics," I don't just mean senators. I mean the way our media works. Kelly interested me in politics when I was younger, but Trudeau explained it. He showed the relationship of the media to the senators and to the lobbyists in a way that was funny and told you more than the actual news told you, because it was true.

It was satire, but there is satire in other media. There is satire on TV. I was reading all that stuff at the same time *All in the Family* was on. But, to this day, I don't think you can find more truth in any other medium than in comics. I think that kind of artist—like a political cartoonist—blows away all the clouds of games and all that kind of stuff and just gets to the stripped-down truth of the matter. I've always felt that way, even as a kid, first with *Mad Magazine* and then with *Pogo*. There was nowhere else you could look and get that kind of truth about what was really going on. You sure couldn't get it from commercials or TV. Most sitcoms and commercials are unbearable to me. I never thought movies were false or anything, but I always felt that movies were really beautiful structured pieces of art that were stories—sort of like novels. Comics were where I was told the truth. That's the only place I could get the truth—*Mad Magazine* and *Pogo* and *Doonesbury* and, really, *Peanuts*. That was real stuff. That was real interaction, there was no hiding. That is how the dirty stuff works. That's reality. Of course Trudeau also developed his own comics pacing, with those four identical panels that he painstakingly redrew with just the smallest facial tic...and the penultimate panel. With those two innovations, he made it to the top pantheon as far as I'm concerned.

**LSC — A lot of people don't think about the writing part of comics. Can you talk about your influences in writing?**

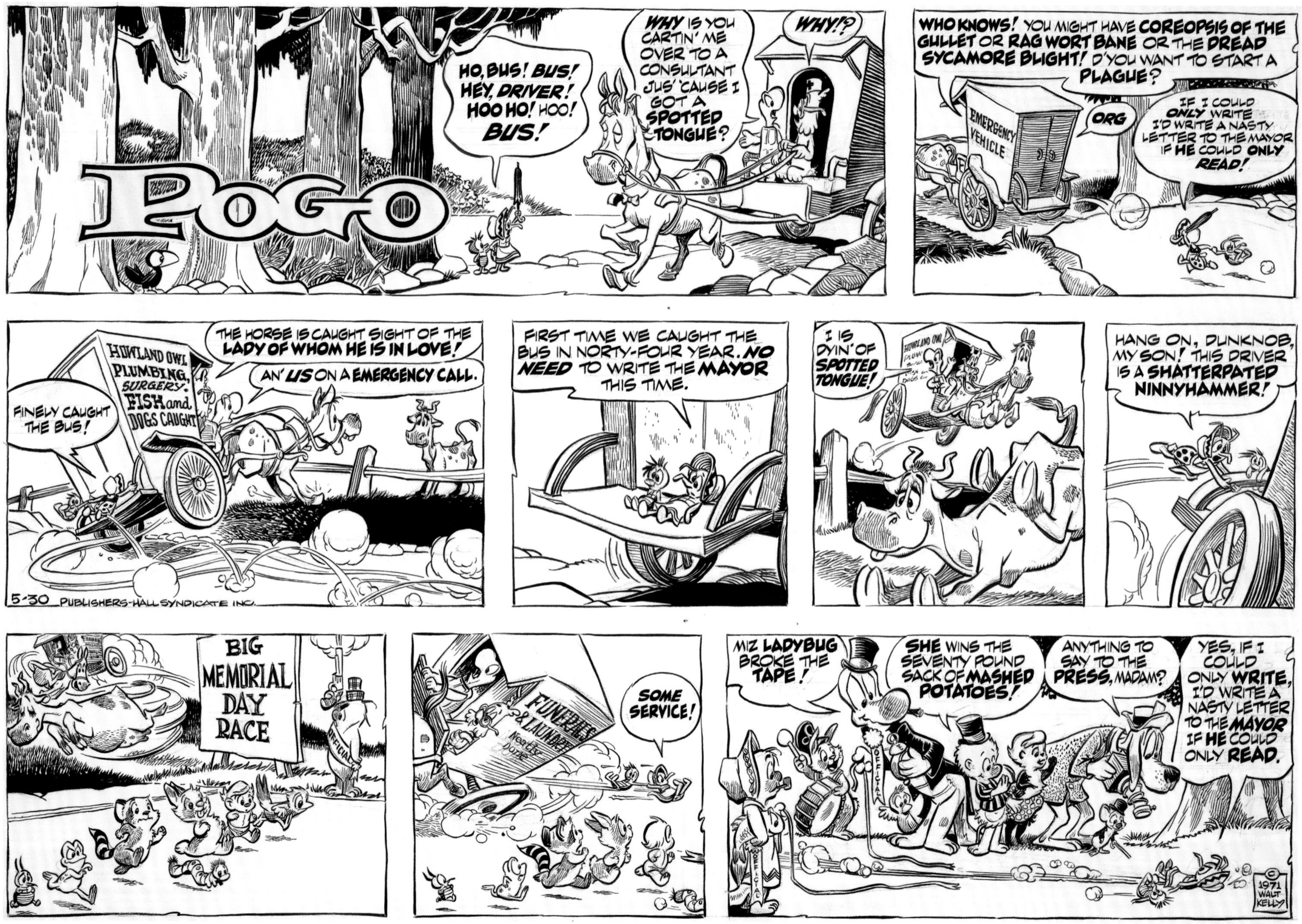
POGO
HO, BUS! BUS! HEY, DRIVER! HOO HO! HOO! BUS!
WHY IS YOU CARTIN' ME OVER TO A CONSULTANT JUS' 'CAUSE I GOT A SPOTTED TONGUE?
WHY!?
WHO KNOWS! YOU MIGHT HAVE COREOPSIS OF THE GULLET OR RAG WORT BANE OR THE DREAD SYCAMORE BLIGHT! D'YOU WANT TO START A PLAGUE?
EMERGENCY VEHICLE
ORG
IF I COULD ONLY WRITE I'D WRITE A NASTY LETTER TO THE MAYOR IF HE COULD ONLY READ!
HOWLAND OWL PLUMBING, SURGERY. FISH and DOGS CAUGHT
FINELY CAUGHT THE BUS!
THE HORSE IS CAUGHT SIGHT OF THE LADY OF WHOM HE IS IN LOVE!
AN' US ON A EMERGENCY CALL.
5-30 PUBLISHERS-HALL SYNDICATE INC.
FIRST TIME WE CAUGHT THE BUS IN NORTY-FOUR YEAR. NO NEED TO WRITE THE MAYOR THIS TIME.
I IS DYIN' OF SPOTTED TONGUE!
HANG ON, DUNKNOB, MY SON! THIS DRIVER IS A SHATTERPATED NINNYHAMMER!
BIG MEMORIAL DAY RACE
OFFICIAL
FUNERALS & LAUNDRY Neatly Done
SOME SERVICE!
MIZ LADYBUG BROKE THE TAPE!
SHE WINS THE SEVENTY POUND SACK OF MASHED POTATOES!
ANYTHING TO SAY TO THE PRESS, MADAM?
YES, IF I COULD ONLY WRITE, I'D WRITE A NASTY LETTER TO THE MAYOR IF HE COULD ONLY READ.
© 1971 WALT KELLY

JS — My biggest influence in writing comics is Walt Kelly. His ability to have dialogue come from different characters in *Pogo*, and have that dialogue grounded in that character's personality, is unrivaled. But also a lot of my writing influences come from outside of comics. I really like a lot of movies, like *Casablanca*—I like that complicated and yet very simple and perfectly formed puzzle that creates a story. I really like things that start off very simple and childlike, like *Huckleberry Finn* or even *The Odyssey*. I can't think of any other examples right now, but as the story goes on the themes become much more complex and adult and dark sometimes. That is the kind of story that I'm drawn to and that I want to try to tell.

When you asked that, I first thought of the kind of writing that doesn't involve words. In comics, you are writing with blocks of panel—blocks of art—that sometimes include word balloons. So to me, as I mentioned earlier, the smallest basic unit of writing in comics is any two given panels, because those two panels play off each other—and then of course the next two panels. So it is always just the two panels leaping over that gutter that creates the writing. What I was talking about with the pacing—making sure the reader's eye doesn't spend too much time on a panel when you don't want it to—all of that goes into writing in comics. The best way to explain this might be to share an example of a time I had a lot of readers mad at me when I did one comic: *Bone* #16, which is in this show. The entire issue is up.

I had a twenty-page comic to do, and I thought it would be fun to try an experiment and to present the comic in real time; that is to say the amount of time it would take the reader to open up the front cover, start reading the comic, and by the time he closes it—say it was fifteen minutes, twenty minutes, or whatever, however long it took them to read that comic—that's how much time it took for the characters inside the story to do whatever they had to do. Since the subject matter was the Bones being chased through a stormy forest, I had all sorts of opportunity to create atmosphere, to try to have suspense, because they didn't know where the monsters were in this dark, stormy forest—all around them or right next to them. They wouldn't know if they were nearby unless there was a lightning flash. So I did an entire twenty-page comic like I just described. There are some words but not a lot. It takes fifteen minutes for them to run through this forest and evade all these monsters, and it takes fifteen minutes to read it. That was a lot of fun to do, and I had a lot of cartoonist friends write me or call me and say that they really dug it—they liked it a lot...it was one of their favorite things. But the readers...oh my gosh, I got so much hate mail. I couldn't believe it. A lot of people thought I was ripping them off because they paid full price for this comic, but there were no words in it. I was really surprised by that. It was an eye-opening experience. Because it took me just as long to draw every panel, whether it had words or not.

DF — **Did comics serve as an escape for you as a kid or as a way of learning about the world around you?**

JS — I think I can honestly say it was both. I would love to get a comic book and then couldn't wait to go sit somewhere and read it. As soon as you start reading, the world's gone. But it was always a way to filter the world I was looking at. That probably comes from *Mad Magazine* and *Pogo*, because *Pogo* was unashamedly a giant metaphor for human foibles and politics. So it was always a way to talk about real life. And to me, that is the art part. That is what makes it art.

Walt Kelly
*Pogo*, May 30, 1971
Ink and blue pencil on paper
16½ x 25¼ in.

**DF** — **You brought up the concept of the auteur in comic strips, the idea of one person drawing and writing the strip. How young were you when you were aware of that?**

**JS** — I think I must have been pretty young, five. I knew that Walt Disney was on TV every Sunday night back in the 1960s and you knew that he made up Mickey Mouse, right? And the same with Walter Lantz who made up Woody Woodpecker, and Charles Schulz with Snoopy. So I think very early on I knew that cartoons had cartoonists. Fone Bone was my early attempt to come up with a Snoopy or a Mickey Mouse or something. I was definitely aware of it very early on.

**DF** — **Were you aware of the distinction between a single artist working on *Peanuts* and, say, a group of people working on a *Superman* comic book?**

**JS** — No, of course not.

**DF** — **Not when you were five, but maybe when you were twelve or thirteen?**

**JS** — In the early days of comics they didn't credit the different artists that came together to make a book. But by the time I was eight or nine, it was starting to be a little more common practice. You knew that Jack Kirby was drawing *Fantastic Four*, and you knew that Neal Adams was drawing *Batman* and *Green Lantern*. By the time I was ten I was seeking out Neal Adams or Joe Kubert on a book. I was looking for that individual artist to follow his progression, because he got better every single issue—it was just so exciting.

**LSC** — **How do you decide what part of the story not to tell versus what you want to tell?**

**JS** — In some cases you can make a dramatic decision that things "off screen," so to speak, have more impact. A famous example is Bambi's mother getting killed. People think that is such a big dramatic, violent event, but it's actually never seen on screen. It takes place when the camera's following Bambi running away. I actually think that adds power and weight to it. I was trying to think of an example of me doing that. I know I did. There is violence in *Bone*, but I only occasionally show it. So sometimes you do that. Other times you make decisions on what is the most interesting. What is the most immediate thing happening? And you have to draw that because that is what engages.

**DF** — **In *Bone* we never see Boneville. We only hear about why the Bones left Boneville.**

**JS** — That kind of falls into the dramatic thing, where you decide that something is going to have more weight if it's not seen. I started to get letters from people saying, "Oh I can't wait to see Boneville." And then they would describe what they thought Boneville looked like. Nobody's descriptions were the same. Some of them were really imaginative. I realized I just wasn't going to show Boneville then because I could tell that it had much more weight for each reader when they made it up themselves. That's one of the problems I've had with Hollywood when they want to start a screenplay. They always want to start in Boneville because it's a much more linear way to start a story. And I just can't. I can't let them. But I think your question really is not about those decisions. You're asking about what do you decide to draw, because if it's a continuum of motion or an action that is going on, what do you pick? And, I don't know. I think about when I used to animate, and you learn to zero in on the key moments that communicate the most.

**DF** — **There are points in the story where two pages could be one drawing. How do you determine what needs to be fully drawn out and emphasized by showing greater detail?**

**JS** — Part of that comes down to process. At some point you move on instinct—like when I'm writing the scripts and I rough them out. As I start to build up the pages, first they're in pencil and then more and more ink, then the lettering goes on…. For each step, I read the panels over and over again, trying to stay with the rhythm that's being created. If you want it to go faster—if it is going too slow—and you feel like the story should hop a little more, you can do things to speed up what's going on. You can take some words out, or take away some detail. Sometimes as your eye moves through a panel, when it's in pencil, the timing looks great. When I ink it, some big solid block or a little piece of detail might catch your eye and slow you down, and you spend a little too much time on that panel—and linger—before you go to the next panel. So in the process, you just have to continue to reread it and refine it and make sure that the speed is all there. Hopefully before you get that far along in the script stage, you'll have caught an extra beat that you don't need and you can get rid of that.

**LSC** — **Can you talk a little bit about the double-page spreads in which you then place smaller panels, the kind of layout Eisner called a "meta-panel"? How do you imagine readers approaching those pages?**

**JS** — Everything has to do with placement. I rarely do a double-page spread. That's when you have the book flat open and the entire surface of the book is a single panel. Sometimes you can set a panel inside that panel. It depends where you put the panel. If you put the little inset panel—a little circle or a little square or whatever—in the upper left, then it is likely going to get looked at first. Because reading comics is identical to reading prose: you start in the upper left and go left to right, top to bottom, just like in any other book. You turn the page, and if there's a panel up there, you, as a Western reader, are automatically going to go up there. So, as an author, you have some choices to make. If you're going to use a double-page spread, you're going to make that choice because you want the impact of a panel that large. This is such a complicated topic.

There is a build-up to a splash page. I normally put about six panels to a page. A lot of people do eight panels to a page. But what you do is establish a rhythm of your six panels a page, and then if, suddenly, a whole page or two pages are used for a larger image, it is going to have an impact. So you've made the decision to use this double-page spread…. Sometimes you might want to set something inside it, sometimes not. It just depends on timing. If it is a big double-page spread of, say, the valley, and that image is timeless, then I may want to have a character speak without putting a balloon in that big, beautiful image. I may put a little panel down there and have the character say something—"Wow, what a great view!"—or maybe something more tied into the story. But that would then imply to me that he was saying that standing there looking out over that valley. The story's not moving on. I want him to be still standing there and for the reader to *feel* that view as he's saying it. Whereas if I wanted the story to move on, if they were confronted by an army or something, and that was the double-page spread conveying a massive size, I might not want to have a character stand there and say anything. I might want to turn the page, and then I wouldn't

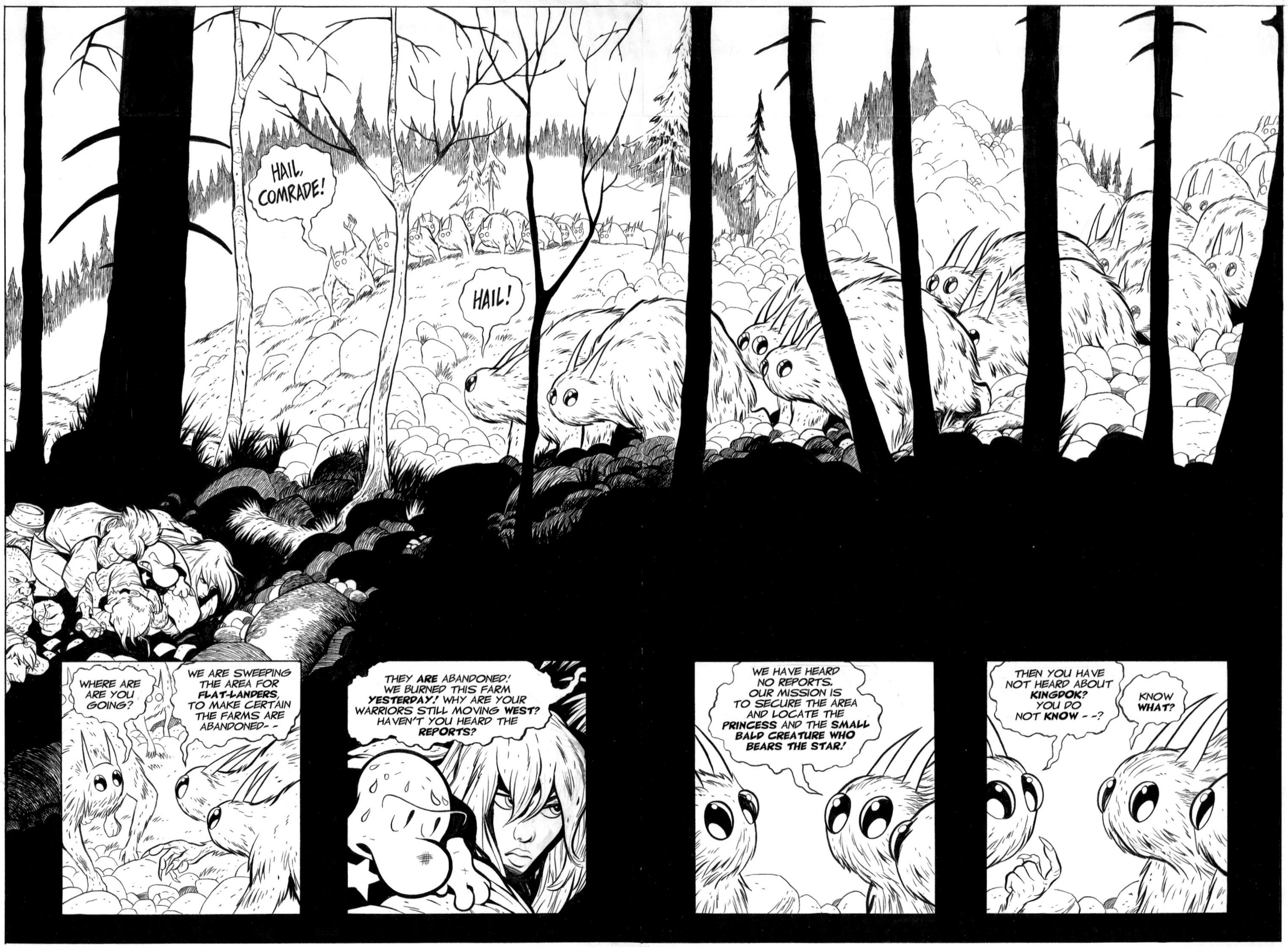
HAIL, COMRADE!
HAIL!
WHERE ARE YOU GOING?
WE ARE SWEEPING THE AREA FOR FLAT-LANDERS, TO MAKE CERTAIN THE FARMS ARE ABANDONED- -
THEY ARE ABANDONED! WE BURNED THIS FARM YESTERDAY! WHY ARE YOUR WARRIORS STILL MOVING WEST? HAVEN'T YOU HEARD THE REPORTS?
WE HAVE HEARD NO REPORTS. OUR MISSION IS TO SECURE THE AREA AND LOCATE THE PRINCESS AND THE SMALL BALD CREATURE WHO BEARS THE STAR!
THEN YOU HAVE NOT HEARD ABOUT KINGDOK? YOU DO NOT KNOW - -?
KNOW WHAT?

use a double-page spread or I wouldn't put any message in there. So it is a question of placement and timing. Do I want people to feel like they're in this image? I never thought about that before. But that's actually totally what you're doing.

DF — **When filmmakers are preparing for a film, they often will go back and watch other directors' films—or maybe tell their cinematographer or art director, "I want you to watch these films" for inspiration. Obviously it's different because you're working by yourself. Maybe you didn't do that with *Bone*, but when you're working on projects now, do you look at other people's work to inform your own?**

JS — I rarely look at comics or comic books for that kind of influence. I *will* look at movies. That is where I go for inspiration on composition of a frame, or even a story structure. I've just been drawn to that kind of thing. That is why I've been always drawn more toward the longer form of comics, because it fits with my notion of story, which has more in common with film and books than with traditional comics, which have always been a very ephemeral art form. Charlie Brown never ages and he goes on and on and on and on. He never even changes his shirt. So just in the last twenty years, really, have comics begun to move into this new kind of storytelling, which is a little more like a novel or like a film—something with a beginning, and a middle, and an end—a structure like that, as opposed to just an open-ended soap opera… like Spiderman never kissing his girlfriend, or whatever.

DF — **You mentioned how comics have changed over the last twenty years or so. One way that *Bone* really stands out from some of the other acclaimed graphic novels, recently anyway, is that so many of them are either autobiographical**

or they're about historical events in one way or another, whereas *Bone* is completely original, fictional, narrative. Why do you think so many people are turning to the graphic novel medium to tell their life stories?

JS — That's a good question. I believe it's rooted in the past of comics, like the traditions that Robert Crumb started. The underground comics were a reaction to the corporate, cleaned-up comics that Robert Crumb was reading in the 1950s. Instead of these packaged comics done by factories, he wanted to do the opposite. He was trying to do real life—his thoughts, his pains—and everything the establishment didn't like, he wanted to put in there. So there is a long tradition in underground comics of autobiographical material. There are also the comics that read like literary fiction, that aren't necessarily autobiography but tales grounded in postmodern life. There are a lot of really good artists working in that genre right now, like Dan Clowes and Chris Ware. I think that if they weren't doing such strong work, there wouldn't be the interest in it. It is also easier for the critics to hold onto it. There's something about working in an office and being alienated in your cubicle… there is a lot more for a critic to hold onto than with fantasy stories with flying monsters and wizards and stuff.

DF — **It's interesting to me how Marjane Satrapi's *Persepolis* books drew multiple articles in the *New York Times*. I think part of it was that they were able to treat it in a different way because it was about political issues and cultural issues. It's almost as if that gave the newspaper a greater license to put it on the front page of the arts section.**

*Bone* 33, pp. 2–3, 1998
(*Bone: The Complete Cartoon Epic in One Volume*, pp. 730–31)
Ink and blue pencil on paper
17 x 14 in., each page

JS——*Persepolis* has multiple hooks because not only is it autobiographical, but it's topical. It's a woman working in a medium where very few women are excelling, and it's about a woman who is writing about Iran, where women are repressed. So you have all kinds of hooks, and it's also really good. That's the kind of thing that hits. I kind of said that all backwards, because what I really meant is it's good, but it also has a hook by being about so many topical things.

DF——**That is not just true for comic books, it is true for, say, film as well. It's kind of ridiculous to use the Academy Awards as an example, but you rarely see a comedy, for instance, winning all the awards. It's usually films about political subjects or other serious subjects.**

JS——*Bone* has been very unusual in that it's had that critical acclaim, and it doesn't fit the mold. I never quite understood what drew critics to it. It started being picked up critically at a time when comics were experiencing a real commercial crush: the collectors' market had taken over and comic publishers were manufacturing "chase" comics—super special comics that you had to order a hundred normal issues in order to get the one that had a fold-out cover. At that time *Bone* emerged as a hand-drawn book being done out of my garage, and at the same time the garage music scene was happening in Seattle. A lot of the critics grabbed on to *Bone* because it was high profile enough that it was something that they could say, "this works." I got lucky that it kind of popped out and got out of the fantasy/comedy rut that it could've gotten stuck in very easily.

LSC——**Why do you think critics don't take fiction more seriously in the graphic novel world?**

JS——I'd like to find that *Time* top ten list to see what is on there.* Most of the choices are like *Blankets* and *Fun Home*… but *Bone*'s not the only fantasy one is it? (JS looks at the *Time* list online.) *David Boring* and *Ed the Happy Clown*. That's crazy stuff. *Jimmy Corrigan, Palomar*. Alan Moore's *Watchmen*, that's superheroes. I'm wondering if it's not quite as bad as it seems. When the very first people go out on a limb to talk about comics in a big publication like *Time* or the *New York Times*, they're going to take something that's a little more staid—something that's a little bit more like what is normally considered a good comic—or a good novel. Looking at the *Time* list, about half of them are unrealistic like *Boulevard of Broken Dreams* or *Happy Clown* or *Bone*. I think with comics, there are certain things that comics do, that comics do *great*—and that you can't do in a novel. Something like *Bone*, you probably could do in a movie, but it's not the same. You can do fantasy things with drawings and convey them better in a comic than you can in a novel. I think that now that comics—graphic novels—have become a little bit more accepted, even just during the last three years, you see that these lists are starting to include things that have more "comicy" subject matter.

LSC——**Can you expand on that to talk about reading graphic novels versus reading a page of print?**

JS——Well, reading has the same rules—left to right, top to bottom. But when you read a comic, some of the information is in the picture. You do have to learn to read the pictures. You can't just look at the word balloons and skip to the next word. You've got to pick up the information and clues that are in the art. Comics have a very specific set of symbols that they've developed over the last sixty years, all their

*In 2005, *Time* magazine online published a list of the "top ten" graphic novels of all time, compiled and annotated by Andrew D. Arnold, the magazine's "comix" columnist. The list was a complement to a similar compilation of 100 English-language novels published since *Time*'s founding in 1923 as selected by critics Lev Grossman and Richard Lacayo. That complete list was also available only online, but a selection of 10 titles and their accompanying notes appeared in the magazine's print issue of October 24, 2005 (106: 112).

Here is Arnold's graphic novels list, which was given in alphabetical order and included only book-length fictional stories originally published in English: *Berlin: City of Stones* by Jason Lutes (2000), the first in a series set in Berlin during the Weimar Republic; *Blankets* by Craig Thompson (2003), a semi-autobiographical account of adolescence; *Bone* by Jeff Smith (2004); *The Boulevard of Broken Dreams* by Kim Deitch (2002), which tells the story of an animator in the 1930s and an evil cat named Waldo; *The Dark Knight Returns* by Frank Miller (1986), which chronicles Batman's latter days with dark comedy; *David Boring* (2002) by Daniel Clowes, an apocalyptic romance; *Ed the Happy Clown* by Chester Brown (1989), a fantasy farce; *Jimmy Corrigan: The Smartest Kid on Earth* by Chris Ware (2002), a tragicomic story about race and family; *Palomar: The Heartbreak Soup Stories* by Gilbert Hernadez (2003), a multigenerational epic set in a south-of-the-border town; *Watchman* written by Alan Moore and drawn by Dave Gibbons (1986), a murder mystery that also "deconstructs" the genre of the superhero.—Ed., Andrew D. Arnold, "The All-TIME Graphic Novels," *Time.com*, October 19, 2005, http://www.time.com/time/2005/100books/0,24459,graphic_novels,oo.html (accessed March 14, 2008).

own, that you do need to know, that's a language unique to comics. Some of the rules are very simple—we all know that when somebody runs they leave a little cloud behind them.

**DF** — **You're often quoted as saying that *Bone* is a Warner Bros.' cartoon meets *Lord of the Rings*, and when you go through *Bone*, I think one similarity to the Warner Bros.' cartoons is how often you include references to things outside of the world of the story, such as the inclusion of *Moby-Dick* or, in a different way, the rat creatures loving quiche. There's a scene early on when Fone is emptying his backpack, and he has comic books in it and financial magazines and things like that. It's not unlike what the Warner Bros.' guys did in *What's Opera, Doc?*—referencing Wagner. They were always referring to current events or popular music or "high" culture or even other Warner Bros.' stars. It just struck me how hard it must have been to keep that balance between very cartoony humor elements within a more serious fantasy world—maintaining humor but then also maintaining the threat that the characters face. And then it builds and builds and builds until it gets to the end of the story.**

**JS** — I think it was just a question of balance. Sometimes it would be very tempting to do something—especially if it was funny—to throw things off. I had to learn when it was appropriate to do so. If I knew a big serious event was coming in the story, I would back off on the cartoony stuff for a little while and bring the tone down, and then I could have a big hit. A good example of that is an eight-page story I did for *Disney Adventures Digest*, the kind of magazine you would find at the grocery store. That was a stand-alone story, but in my mind it was going to fit in with the continuity so that later when I collected the books for

the graphic novel I could put it in there. The story was very cartoonlike, about the two Bone cousins, Fone Bone and Phoney Bone, finding a treasure map and following it. In four pages they get more beat up than in any other sequence I ever did—falling off cliffs and getting picked up by giant birds—and in the end it turns out that when they find the treasure, their dirty laundry is in there because Thorn had planted the treasure map since she knew she couldn't get them to do their laundry. It was a funny little bit and when it came time to put it into the books, it came right before a huge dramatic moment in the overall *Bone* story, where Fone Bone pulls out the little map that he found out in the desert. It turns out when he pulls that map out, we learn that it was drawn by Thorn. It proves that she has this past that's been hidden from her and the dragons are real. It really sets the whole story into motion—the whole rest of the story.

When I printed that book, which was, I believe, the third *Bone* collection—in 1995, I think—I sat down, after the books were published, and read it. It didn't fit. On one page, there is a big *Mad Mad Mad Mad World* chase adventure, and then on the next page, Fone Bone pulls this map out of his backpack and initiates the most dramatic part of the story to date. I said, "oh my gosh…I completely undercut it in so many ways." First of all, it's a treasure map, and I just made fun of all maps. So now he pulls out a treasure map, and the whole idea of finding a map has been turned into a cartoon joke. It was a completely silly, ridiculous story where they couldn't be killed no matter how many cliffs they fell off. All danger and drama were shown to be not real. They can't be harmed. So I had to reprint the books and take that story out. That story just floats now and has no real home. That was a really long answer to your questions, but that's exactly what it is: you have to have balance. If there's comedy in the wrong place, it hurts it. But as long as it's in the right place, I think it actually gives the story speed and lightness that it really needs.

**DF—Introducing the whole *Moby-Dick* element is quite a digression. I'm wondering what the reaction has been over the years from fans. It's obviously something that's very important to you. It is something that you really wanted to be part of the story. It fits nicely with the cave where they're having the dreams, but it carries so much meaning with it—the characters from *Moby-Dick*. How did you decide to include it?**

JS—In the beginning it was a comedy element, and it was part of that Warner Bros.' nature of things that come from another world. I wanted Fone Bone to have things from this world because I wanted to impart to the readers that Boneville is like here. Part of the hook of *Bone* is that the humans are the fantasy and the cartoon characters are the reality. We identify with these little cartoony people as opposed to the humans. But as the joke went on, it began to carry some weight and filled a need: that the story had to show Fone Bone's inner life and his inner journey. It was perfect for that because it clearly meant something to the character in the story and it also is based on a book that is layered with symbolism. I thought that was a neat trick to use *Moby-Dick* to show the symbolic layers in *Bone*. It became a signpost.

**DF—Bartleby the rat cub refers to Melville too.**

JS—Yeah, it's just another reference.

**LSC—Can you talk about character development?**

JS—At first a character pops up, and you do need to work on a little background so that the character has some experience to build on. What I discovered is that I would bring in Gran'ma Ben, I knew her. I knew what kind of character she was, and I knew her personality. But as time passed she would grow and change. That new growth would reflect on her backstory. I created a backstory for her. She was the queen at one time and was hiding her granddaughter, à la *Sleeping Beauty*, in the woods to keep her safe. But that backstory necessitated certain personality traits. For example, she was very secretive—and uncommunicative. She had to be because she couldn't tell anybody about

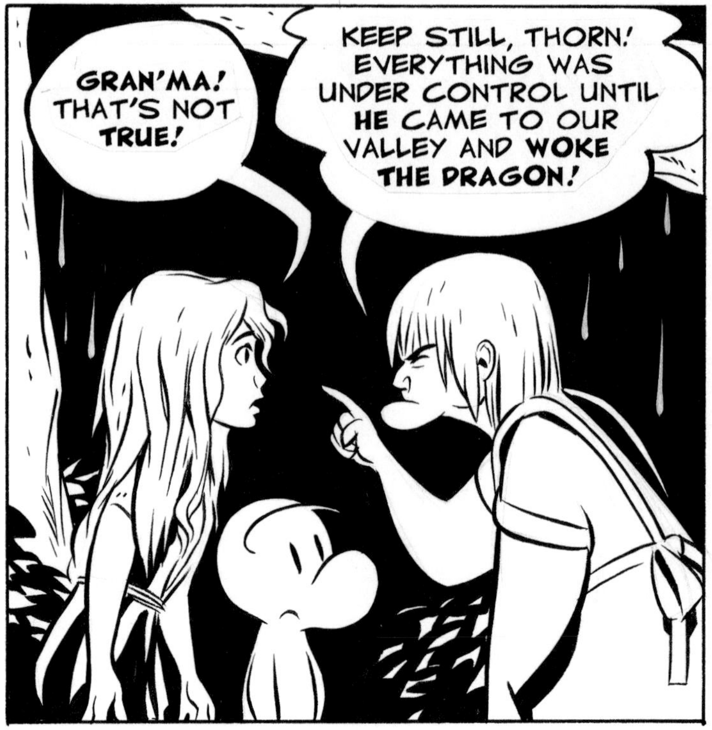
GRAN'MA! THAT'S NOT TRUE!
KEEP STILL, THORN! EVERYTHING WAS UNDER CONTROL UNTIL HE CAME TO OUR VALLEY AND WOKE THE DRAGON!

this, including Thorn. That led to her being this kind of overprotective character, which fed into her strength. So I guess the development comes a little bit intellectually. You have to build, you have to write a backstory for the character.

**DF** — **To follow up on that, it is amazing how quickly you become hooked on the characters in *Bone*. In the first fifteen pages, readers are presented with these characters that look very similar, they're simply drawn characters, and you're immediately concerned about what's going to happen to them.**

**JS** — That goes back to Schulz, too. In Schulz the characters pretty much look the same with just very small cues—costume cues—to tell you who they are. And with almost no ink the absolutely complete and complex range of human emotions is on every one of those *Peanuts'* characters' faces. But for you to just be able to pick up the story and read it and within just the first fifteen pages to know everybody, that's what you have to do when you're telling a story. You have to write it. I knew I had my three character types who were classic comedy types—you know, Groucho, Harpo, and Chico; Mickey, Donald, and Goofy; Jerry Seinfeld, George Costanza, and Kramer. I mean that type is something we all know, which has worked in comedy. But in order to engage the readers as quickly as possible, you have to set up a scenario and a back-and-forth dialogue that pull the readers in and let them know who the characters are and give them situations to show their good and their bad sides, and their funny sides and sympathetic sides. That's just work. I wrote that first fifteen pages fifteen times, definitely, until I felt like the characters came across quick and clean—and that all that work was invisible. When you look at the *Mona Lisa*, you don't see all those layers that add to the depth

and to the glow of the painting. You don't see that. You just look at it and go, "That's the best painting I've ever seen!"

**DF** — **I read an interview with Charles Schulz and he said he thinks people are born with the ability to draw or they're not. He said you can work at it and you can improve your technique, but like singing, you're either able to do it or you're not. Do you agree with that?**

**JS** — Yeah, I do to a degree. I think it's a lot like a musical instrument, and you either have a predilection for it or you don't. And you have the patience and the drive to get better at it or you don't. I think that's actually probably very true. I do not think I could be a musician no matter how much I tried.

**DF** — ***Shazam!* was a change of pace after *Bone*, in that you were writing for very well-known characters, like Captain Marvel, who have quite a bit of history. How did you get involved in the project and did you have any initial concerns about working with such iconic characters?**

**JS** — I got involved with *Shazam!* when the owners of the character, DC Comics, asked me to work on it. I think they felt the whimsy and drawing style of my *Bone* comics would fit the Big Red Cheese. I did have concerns. That character is loved by lots of people and I knew it would be difficult to please everyone, but I approached the project methodically. I researched the early comics and movie serials looking for the flavor and rhythms of the original stories, trying to figure out what it was that made Captain Marvel the most popular comic book character of the Golden Age in the 1940s and 50s. In the end, I decided it was the simple magical transformation of a small, helpless child into a super-being, able to bounce bullets off his chest and fly.

*Bone* 16, p. 5 (detail), 1994
(*Bone: The Complete Cartoon Epic in One Volume*, pp. 357, detail)
Ink and blue pencil on paper
17 x 14 in.

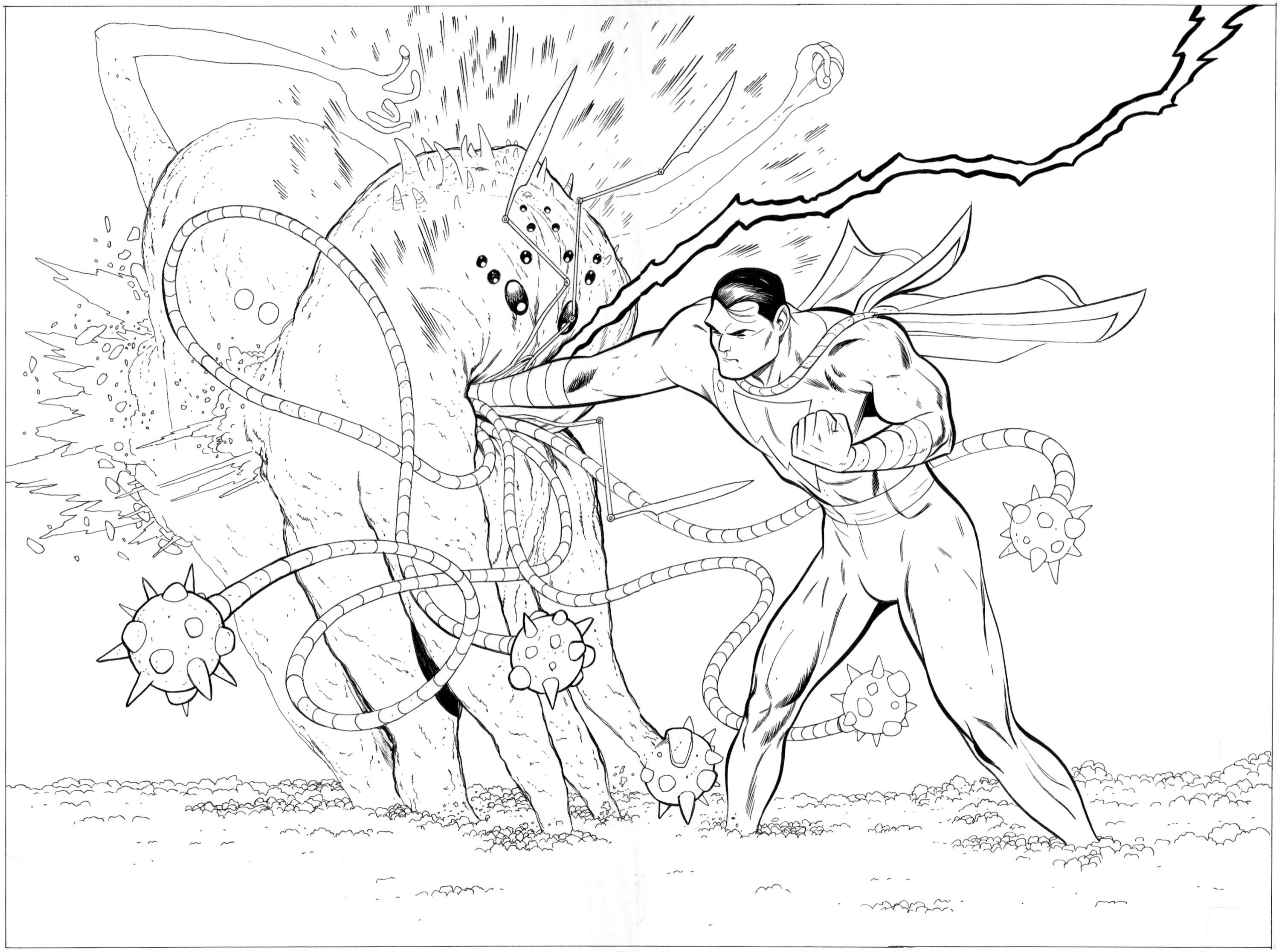

**LSC** — **To come back to the whole idea of inspiration, can you talk about *Rasl* and the inspiration for that?**

JS — *Rasl* is a story of an art thief—a guy whose life is not good. He's very discontented. I guess it's very important to point out that he's an interdimensional art thief. He has invented this spectral immersion suit, which includes large jet engines that he straps to his shoulders and his knees so that he can step in between universes, which he does for money. If someone's rich enough and they want the *Mona Lisa*, he'll go into another dimension and steal the *Mona Lisa*. Rasl is very expensive. The inspiration for an idea like this is that I was interested in writing a comic about a character who is deplorable, as opposed to *Bone*, where the main character is very admirable and doesn't really think bad thoughts. He's not perfect, but he's basically a good guy. I wanted to do one where the hero was kind of a scoundrel. Another element of the interdimensional travel is that in order to operate these jet engines, and to successfully navigate in between the dimensional walls of the universes, Rasl, the main character, has to focus and concentrate and empty his mind—and have almost zenlike peace. However, the process of coming out of it is blinding white and hot and painful in a way that most humans wouldn't be able to take. So when he wakes up in the other dimension, he's on the floor screaming, and it takes him days to recover. And there is a lot of drinking and smoking and gambling and whoring. Once he gets done with that, and gets that all out of his system, he gets to work on his next art theft. Then he has to start the process over again...in order to return, he has to undo all this. He has to cleanse himself—cleanse his body physically—no more smoking, no more drinking. So that's his life—stepping

*Shazam: The Monster Society of Evil*, 4, pp. 34–35, 2007
Ink and blue pencil on paper
Two joined panels,
17⅛ x 28⅛ in., together
Collection of the artist


THROUGH PAGE 30
*Rasl* Preview, pp. 1–6, 2007
Ink and blue pencil on paper
17 x 14 in., each page
Collection of the artist

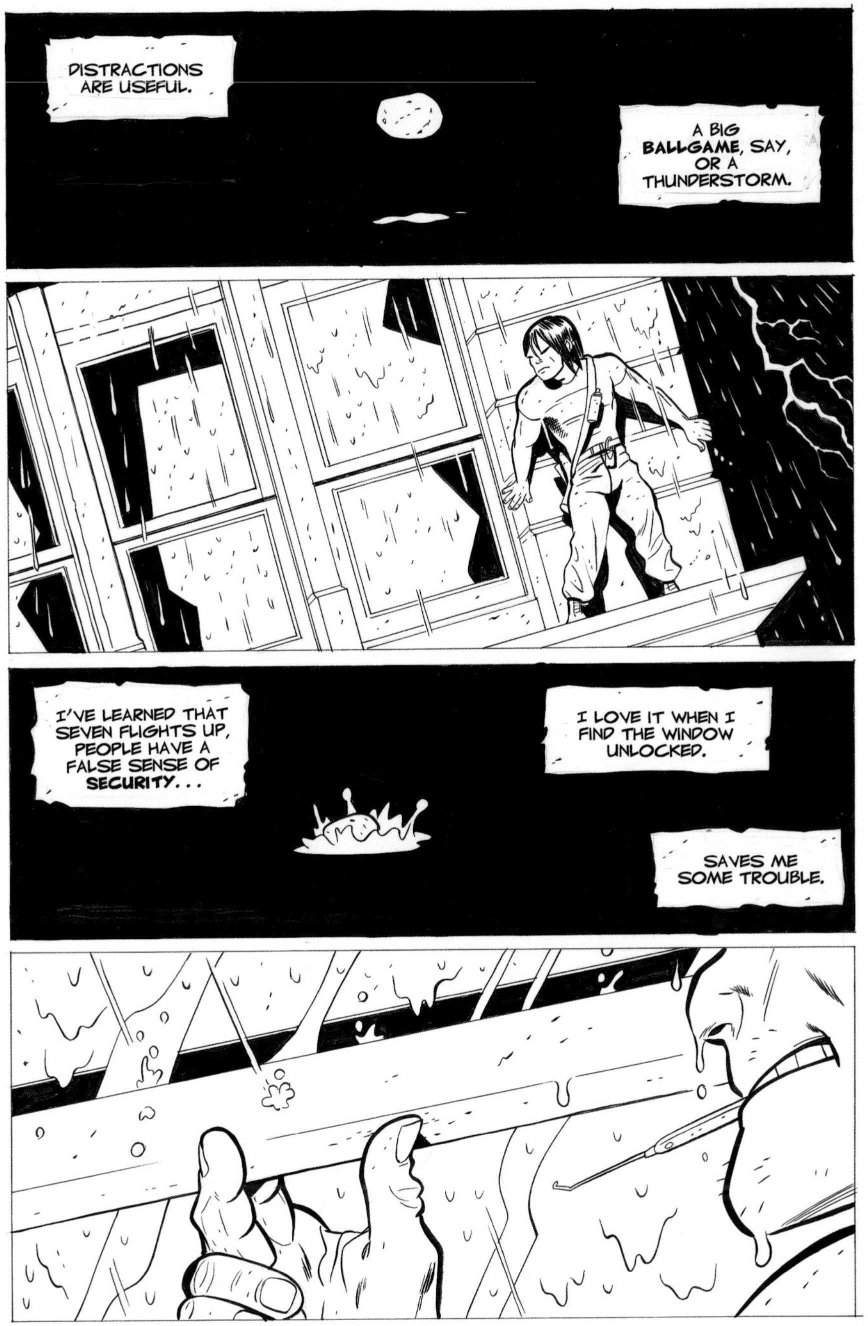
DISTRACTIONS ARE USEFUL.
A BIG BALLGAME, SAY, OR A THUNDERSTORM.
I'VE LEARNED THAT SEVEN FLIGHTS UP, PEOPLE HAVE A FALSE SENSE OF SECURITY...
I LOVE IT WHEN I FIND THE WINDOW UNLOCKED.
SAVES ME SOME TROUBLE.

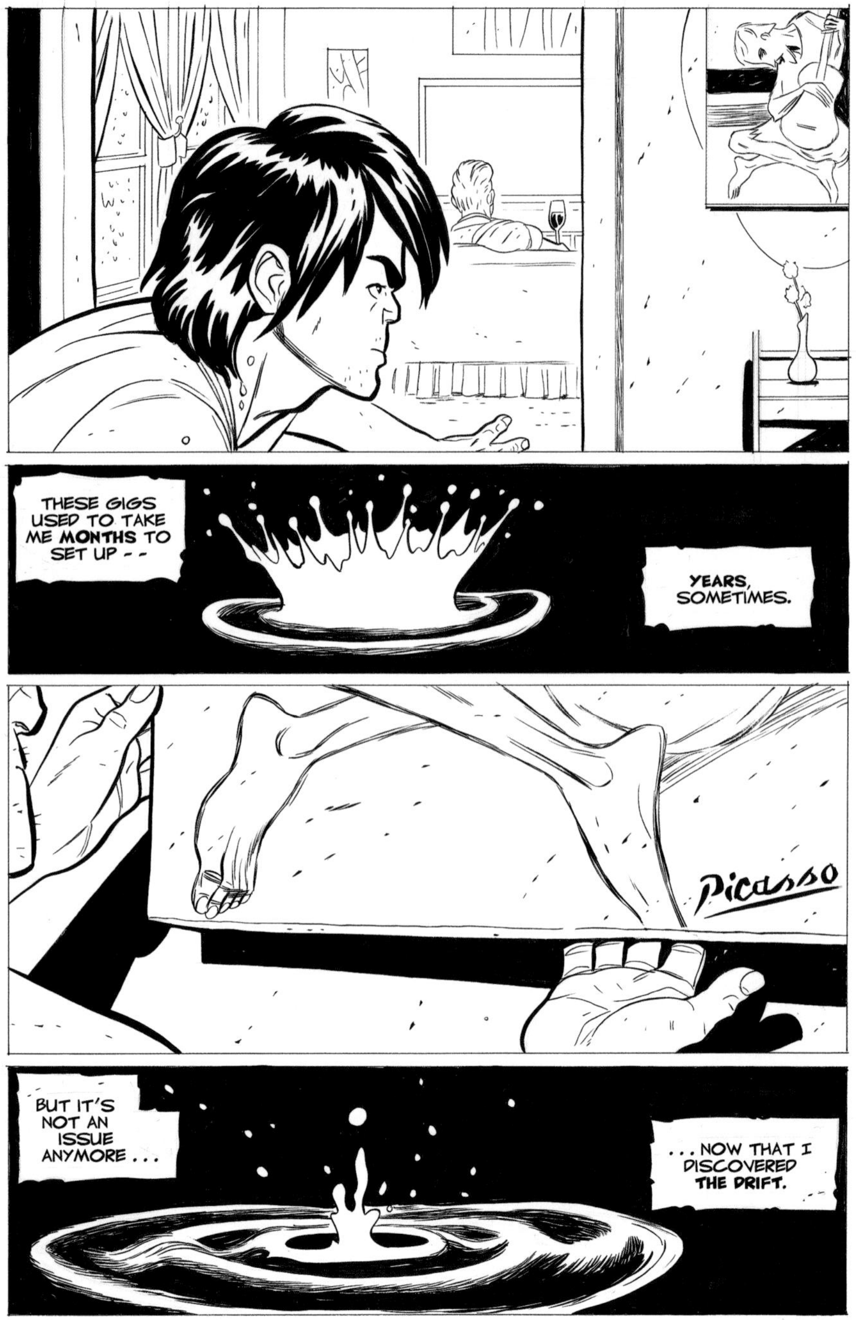
THESE GIGS USED TO TAKE ME **MONTHS** TO SET UP --
**YEARS**, SOMETIMES.
Picasso
BUT IT'S NOT AN ISSUE ANYMORE...
...NOW THAT I DISCOVERED **THE DRIFT.**

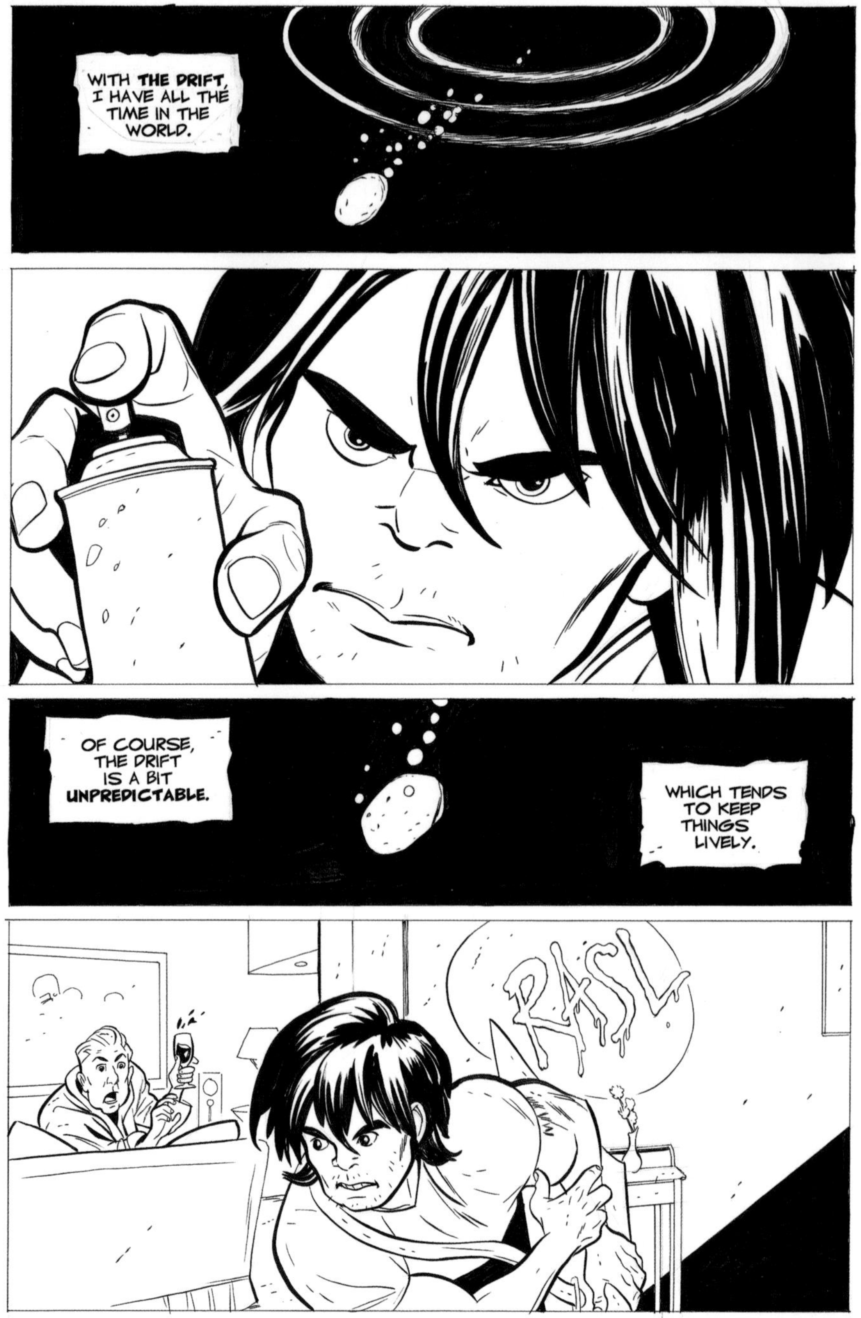
WITH **THE DRIFT**, I HAVE ALL THE TIME IN THE WORLD.
OF COURSE, THE DRIFT IS A BIT **UNPREDICTABLE.**
WHICH TENDS TO KEEP THINGS LIVELY.
RASL

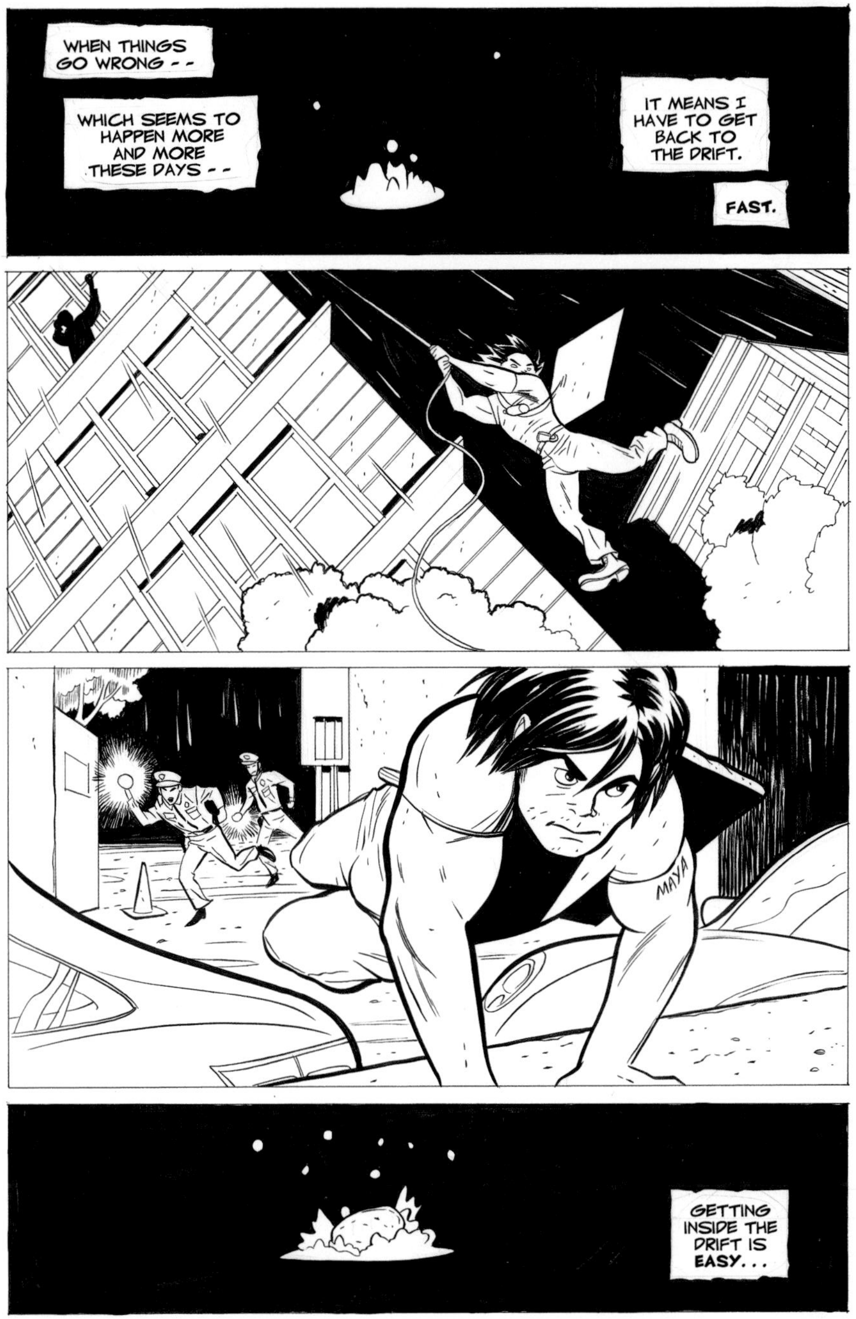
WHEN THINGS GO WRONG - -
WHICH SEEMS TO HAPPEN MORE AND MORE THESE DAYS - -
IT MEANS I HAVE TO GET BACK TO THE DRIFT.
FAST.
MAYA
GETTING INSIDE THE DRIFT IS EASY. . .

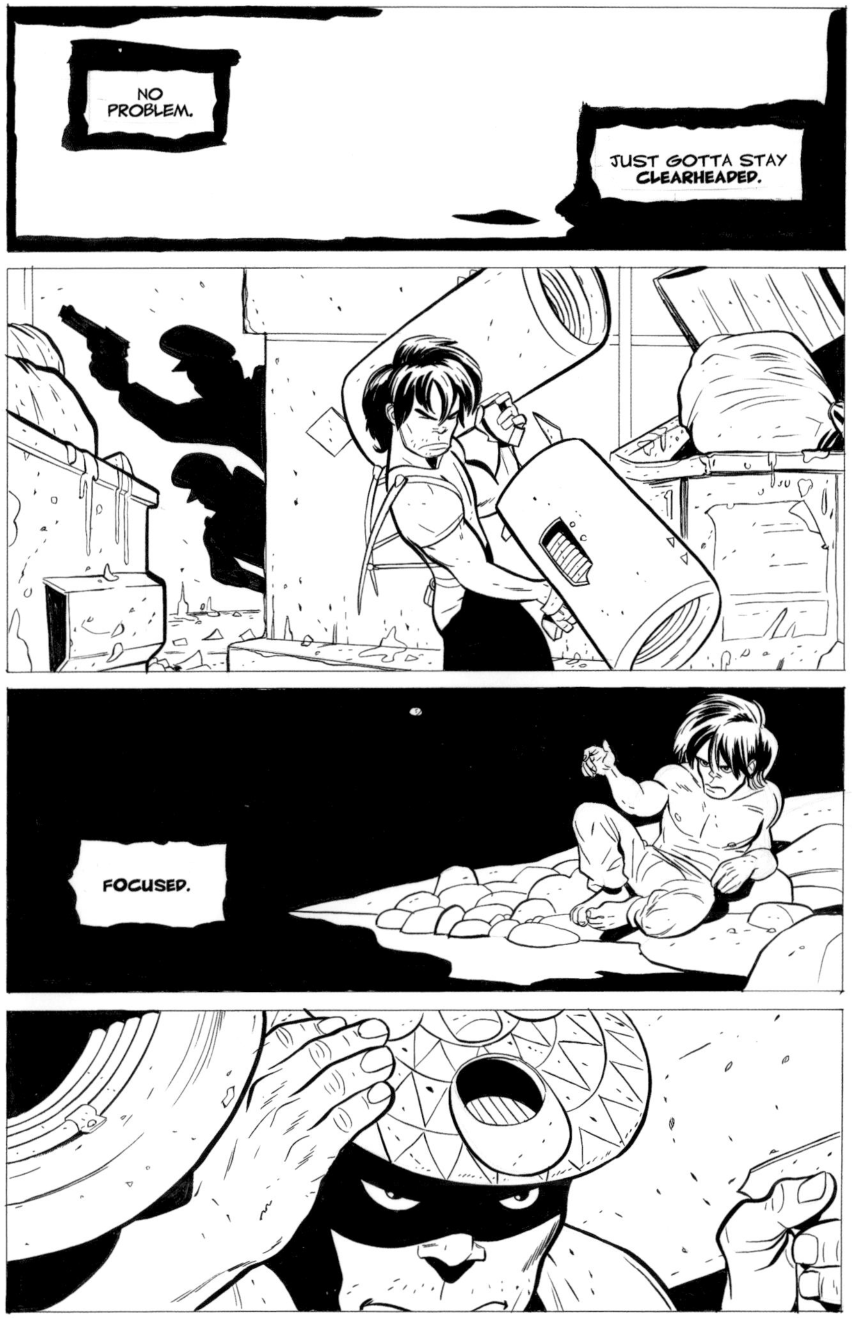
NO PROBLEM.
JUST GOTTA STAY CLEARHEADED.
FOCUSED.

YEAH, GETTING INSIDE IS A PIECE OF CAKE.

IT'S COMING BACK OUT THAT DOES THE DAMAGE . . .

HELL OF A WAY TO MAKE A LIVING.

through this barrier. He goes into it clean and focused, and when he comes out of it he's a screaming wreck in pain. I'm not sure where the inspiration for that came from, but I do know that when I described the project to my wife, her first reaction was, "Oh, that's about the artistic process because that's what you're like every time you start a project and come out of it." Except for the gambling and whoring part. So who knows where these inspirations come from.

**DF —— Were there any other time-traveling works that have had a big influence on you?**

JS —— No. Although I probably will try to look at some good time stories that exist out there. And the best ones are in *Star Trek*. But the time travel's not a huge element. It's more metaphysical. I'm very interested in physics, and string theory, and multiple universes. I have a good science-fiction centerpiece for this story: light is solid. If light is solid, that explains why light behaves as particles and as waves. It also explains why the speed of light is constant, because it doesn't really move. It's kind of like a giant surrounding essence. It's instantaneous. It explains all sorts of other little phenomenon. I thought it was a nice little nugget to have as a science-fiction artifact at the story's center even though it's completely nonsensical and not real. But that's Rasl's big discovery that allows him to do what he does and to step through dimensions.

Most of my influences for *Rasl* are what I'm reading, like Stephen Hawking, Carl Sagan, all the literature that's out there that talks about the furthest, craziest ideas we have about multiple dimensions and that sort of thing. I love all that stuff. Rasl will soon begin to wonder if the dimensions he's traveling to—he's stealing from—are real, or if he's creating them by going to them.

DF — **When you're creating something that you know several different age groups are going to be reading, what things do you have to take into account? What considerations do you have to make? Or do you not even think about it, you're just trying to make the best story that you can?**

JS — I definitely don't categorize what's appropriate for one level and what's appropriate for another level. I just was always turned on by the kinds of stories that worked that way. Bugs Bunny cartoons—or even Disney feature films—work on both levels. One of the reasons parents can take their children to them is because the parents kind of like them, too. I mentioned *Huckleberry Finn* before and *Star Wars*—both of those are stories that are really pretty much for 10-year-old boys, right? They start off with Huck or Luke Skywalker, and they're swashbuckling, but as Huck goes on or as the *Star Wars* movies progressed, they became more sophisticated— became more complex. And the stories had themes that were darker or about dealing with your father, in both *Huckleberry Finn* and *Star Wars.* So it is those kinds of stories that get me excited, and that I want to try to do. I actually might have to wrestle with this a little bit more in *Rasl* than I did in *Bone* because *Rasl* does involve some more failings of the flesh type of subject matter. At this point I haven't actually started writing it yet, so I'm not sure where it's going to go. But my natural inclination as a writer is to tell adventure stories that operate for general audiences. We'll have to see. If Rasl smokes and drinks too much, it may end up being a more adult work. But I don't know that yet. We'll have to see.

DF — **In reading about you and other cartoonists, I'm always struck by how so many, almost without exception, seem to have a really strong sense of the people that came before them. In your work you really get a sense of the people that you're influenced by, where I'm not sure you get the same sense of that when you're reading somebody's more autobiographical story, for instance. I'm wondering if you have a sense that, in a way, we're talking about two different traditions. There is more of a cartoonist tradition, where people are a little bit more acutely aware of artists like Winsor McCay and Herriman, Will Eisner, Jack Kirby, up until the present day, versus people that maybe aren't as interested in that trajectory, and that sequential art just happens to be the art that they're good at—as opposed to painting or...**

JS — No. I think that Harvey Pekar, Robert Crumb, Art Spiegelman, and all those guys are unbelievably aware, and I would say even obsessed, with the tradition of cartooning that came before them. And Chester Brown. All those guys do absolutely feel like they can trace their roots through comics history, through Crumb, through Harvey Kurtzman, through George Herriman—very much the same way I would.

But I don't feel any need to conform to any rules of comics, as far as the industry or format is concerned. I broke many rules repeatedly and was told all along that everything I was doing was undermining everything that is good for comics, like collecting my books into graphic novels and putting them out while my number one was worth $300. People said, "If you do that, then you're going to make the number one comic worthless because you just made it available in a cheap format forever, and if you do that then the retailers are going to hate you because that's where they make their real money, in the back issues." So I was told you can't do graphic novels, you can't do collections, and I just didn't care about any of that stuff. So when it comes to the artwork, I am deeply indebted and in awe of everybody who came before me. But in terms of traditions and industry, I haven't the slightest interest at all in that.

**DF** — **Imagine a teenage girl or boy who might be completely unaware of the history and tradition of comic books. Yet, instead of writing in a journal they create a graphic record of what they're going through, completely outside of the trajectory we've been discussing.**

JS — There may be a generation right now…we call it the indie comics…where people are getting into it who may not have grown up reading certain people—or even knowing who they are. But these artists see the medium in a new way, which is very exciting to me, because even just ten years ago it seemed impossible that the medium could be so well known that people would flock to it and think that it is a place that they could do their art. But that could be happening now. And if it is, I would be excited.

**LSC** — **What do you think about the whole conundrum—how do you learn your craft and your art if you don't have a way to judge what is good and not good and the traditions on which the genre is based?**

JS — I actually think that's why most cartoonists who have come from comic books know the traditions. I mean, the ones that don't know them, really study them, and those who aren't dedicated to that level are going to drop off. You know that's going to happen. But the guys that make it, like Craig Thompson, they know what they're drawing. They've been reading comics, and they're picking the stuff that's good, and they're usually extremely knowledgeable about world comics—not just the stuff you can buy at the grocery store.

They have to be, because you can't go to school to become a comic book artist. Well, I guess you can now. But it's rare. It is still up to the cartoonists to learn it themselves by finding the examples that turn them on. And, boy, they have them now. There's every kind of comic. There are autobiographical comics, comics about world geopolitics…

We're at a time in comics that is completely unlike any that has gone before, where we have a radical shift that involves many elements. There's the graphic novel, which started about twenty years ago with *Maus* and *The Dark Knight Returns* and has really come into flower recently with the wholesale acceptance of graphic novels by large chain bookstores like Barnes & Noble, Borders, and Amazon.com. There's also the element of the Internet, which takes the idea of underground comics and indie comics, which I just mentioned, to a whole new level. You don't even have to figure out how to get your comic books distributed or printed. All you have to do is understand your tools and your technology, and you can upload. There is a large and very healthy community that communicates with each other on the Internet. And the Internet is developing its own sets of symbols and languages that incorporate all that went before it.

The teenager you mentioned a minute ago, creating her graphic diary in her room, is exposed to all these things. The introduction of this new technology so deeply into our lives is making that change. I meet people all the time who are on the fan sites. Another element that's changing comics as we speak is manga, which has more in common with traditional American comics like superheroes, in my opinion, because of the factory nature of the production. Manga are commercial products, designed to sell numbers. For the most part there is an artist and a writer assigned to create a product, although there are auteurs who transcend that. But the numbers are unprecedented. Manga are now at least fifty percent of all comics published in the U.S.—if not sixty, and the numbers are just growing. Manga are turning comics into a mass medium on the level of bestsellers, paperbacks, TV, movies. So we're at a really interesting time. And I'll add one more element that is happening right now, and that's the acceptance by teachers, librarians, and the art world of this as an art form.

LSC — **Another component is the fact that manga have appealed to young girl readers. Comic books have historically appealed to boys. And these people are going to grow up. And I think as they grow up they're going to be a new generation of consumers for this art form in a way that we haven't had before.**

JS — And I'm very excited about it. I think that there are artists getting into this field every day and finding just what you're saying: that it's a fairly natural way to communicate—putting all the words and pictures together. I think that by the time this generation of manga artists grows up, the art is going to be there for everybody. That made me think of an Art Spiegelman story. I think I heard him tell it when he was speaking at Ohio State one time. He was describing the process of ingesting a comic, that these words and picture combinations that are almost instantaneously swallowed into your id through both sides of your brain, that the word and picture bursts that go down before your defenses can stop them, and they're in. I think that was one of the things that excites me about comics—as a kid and now as an artist using that medium. It reaches both sides of your brain and goes in deep and fast and is absorbed into your system almost before your conscious level can filter it. It's that fast. It's dangerous.

This conversation took place at Jeff Smith's studio in Columbus on July 9, 2007.

Transcription by Katie Popoff.

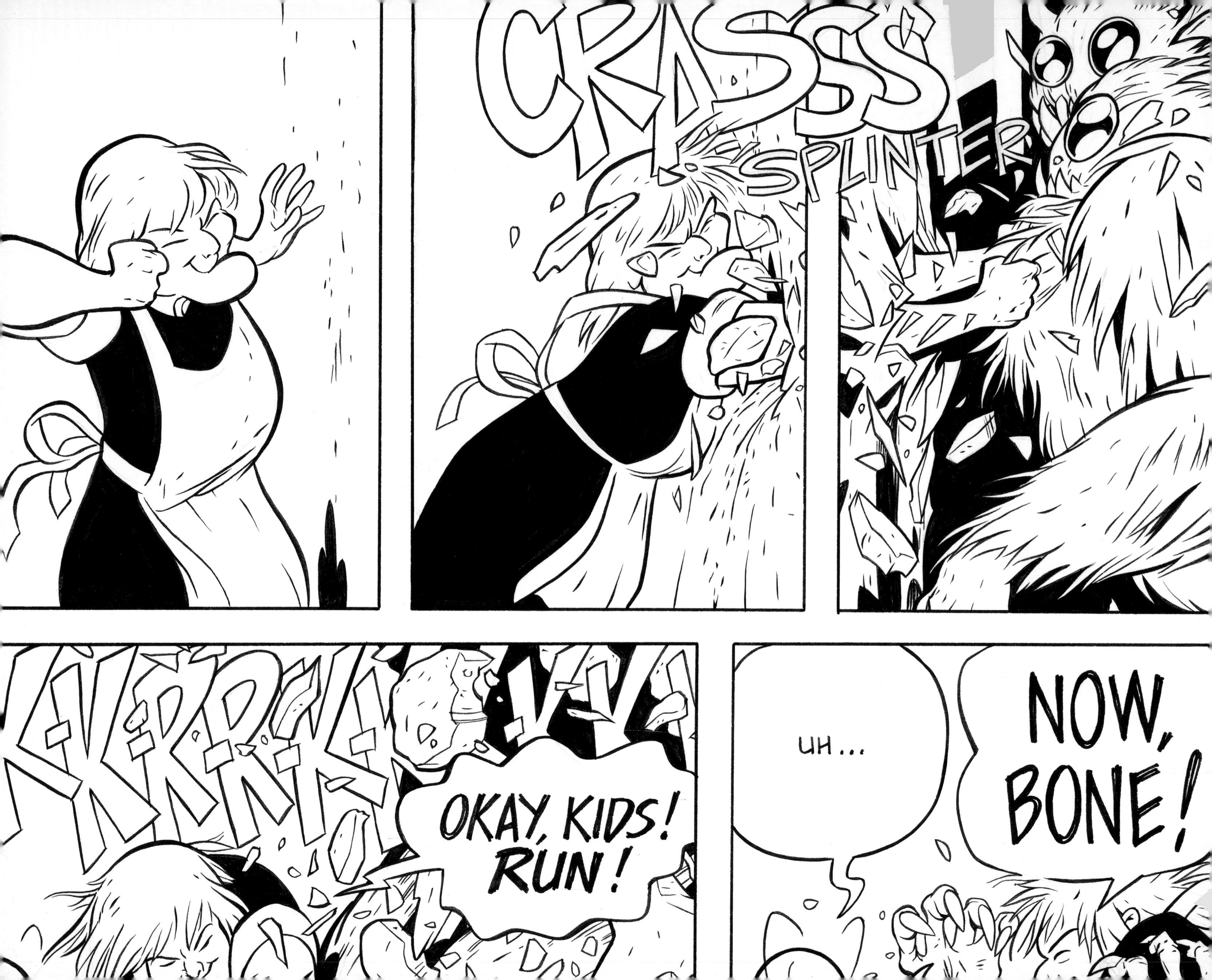
CRASSS
SPLINTER
OKAY, KIDS! RUN!
uh...
NOW, BONE!

## Eyes of the Storm
### Bone 16

One of the most radical and innovative sections of *Bone* was the thunderstorm sequence initially published as issue sixteen in October 1994 and discussed in this catalogue on pages 3, 17, and 82. In *Bone: The Complete Cartoon Epic in One Volume* the sequence is Chapter V, "Eyes of the Storm," in Book Three, *Eyes of the Storm*. The complete artwork for issue sixteen is presented in the exhibition and on the pages that follow. Here, the sequence is introduced by color and black and white cover artwork. It continues with the original art for each page, with some individual panels enlarged to reveal greater detail.

*Bone* 5, p. 3 (detail), 1992
(*Bone: The Complete
Cartoon Epic in One Volume*,
p. 109, detail)
Ink and blue pencil on paper
17 x 14 in.

*Bone* 16, cover, color, 1994
Ink, airbrush and colored
pencils with acetate overlay;
airbrush by David Reed
17 x 14 in.

OVERLEAF
*Bone* 16, cover, black and
white (detail), 1994
Ink and blue pencil on paper
17 x 14 in.

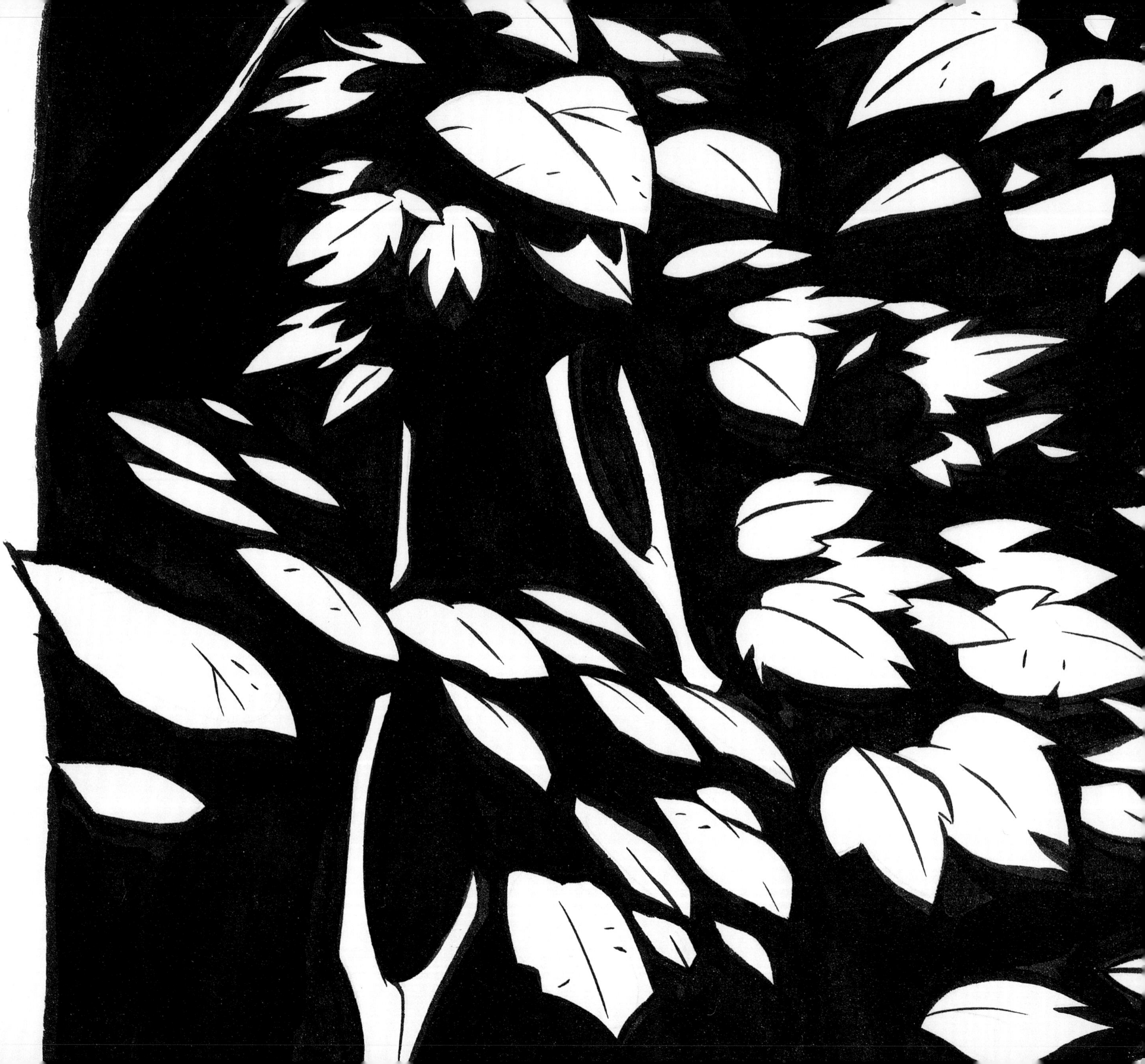

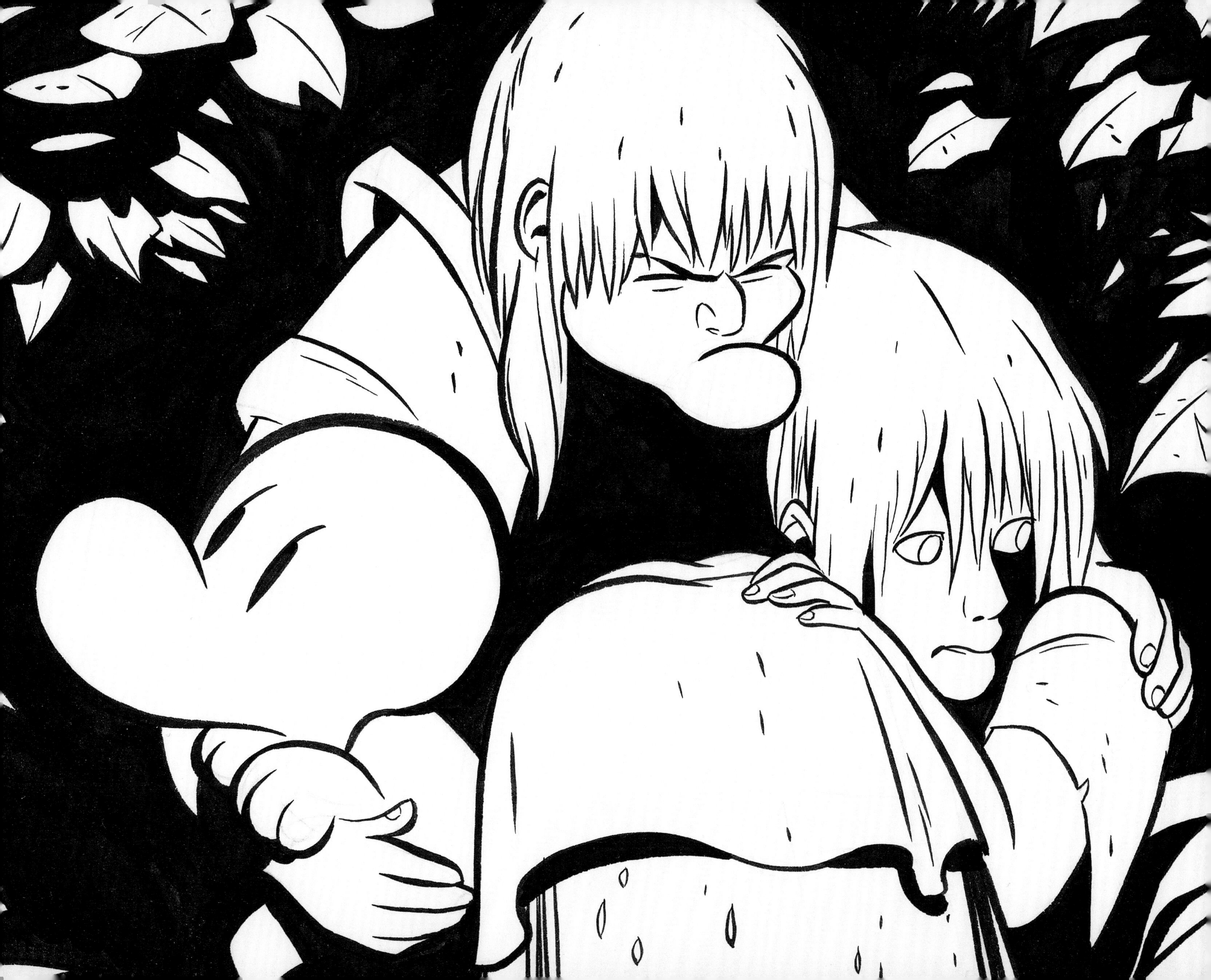

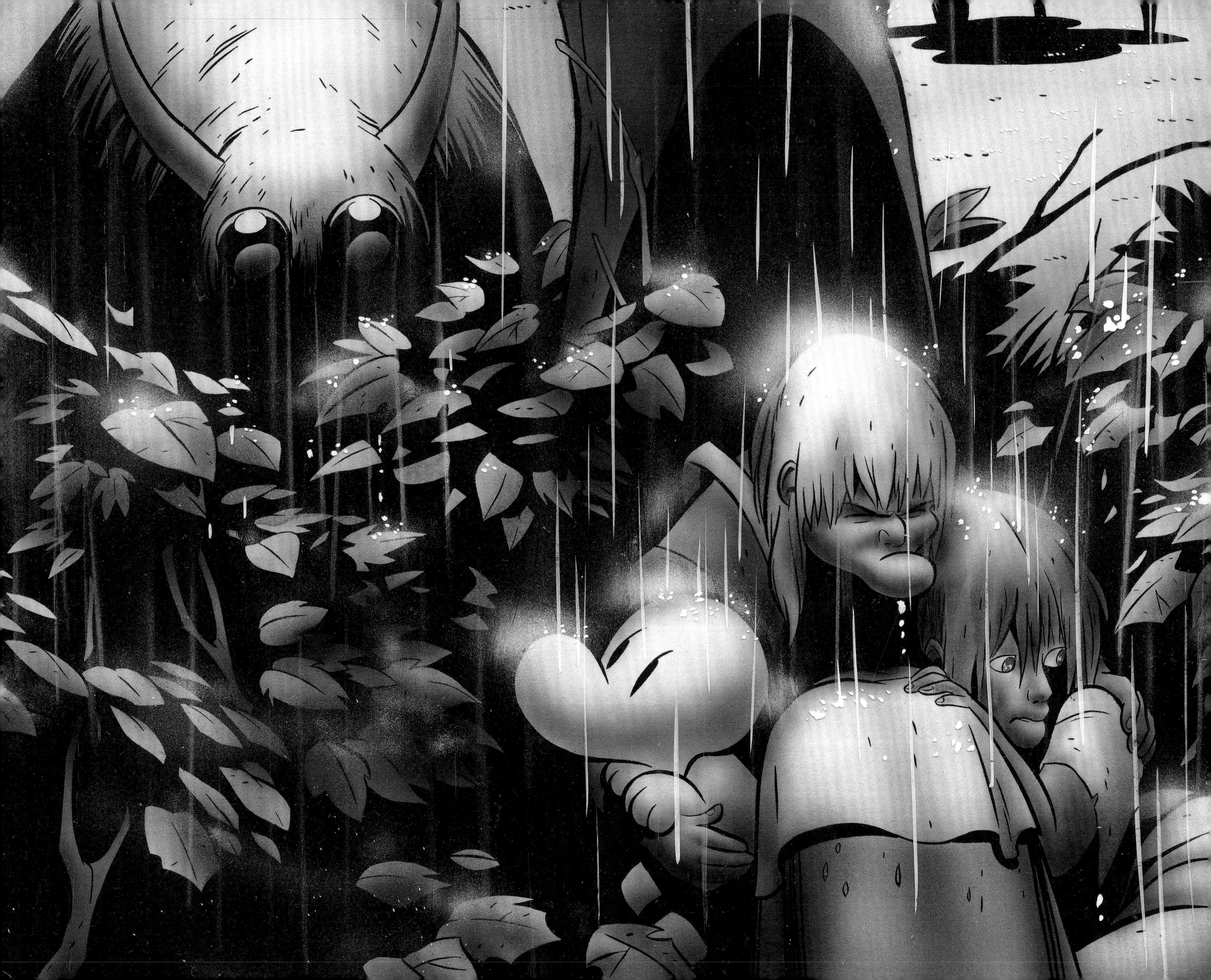

*Bone* 16, cover, color (detail), 1994
Ink, airbrush and colored pencils with acetate overlay; airbrush by David Reed
17 x 14 in.

THROUGH PAGE 61
*Bone* 16, pp. 1–20, 1994
(*Bone: The Complete Cartoon Epic in One Volume*, pp. 353–372)
Ink and blue pencil on paper
17 x 14 in., each page

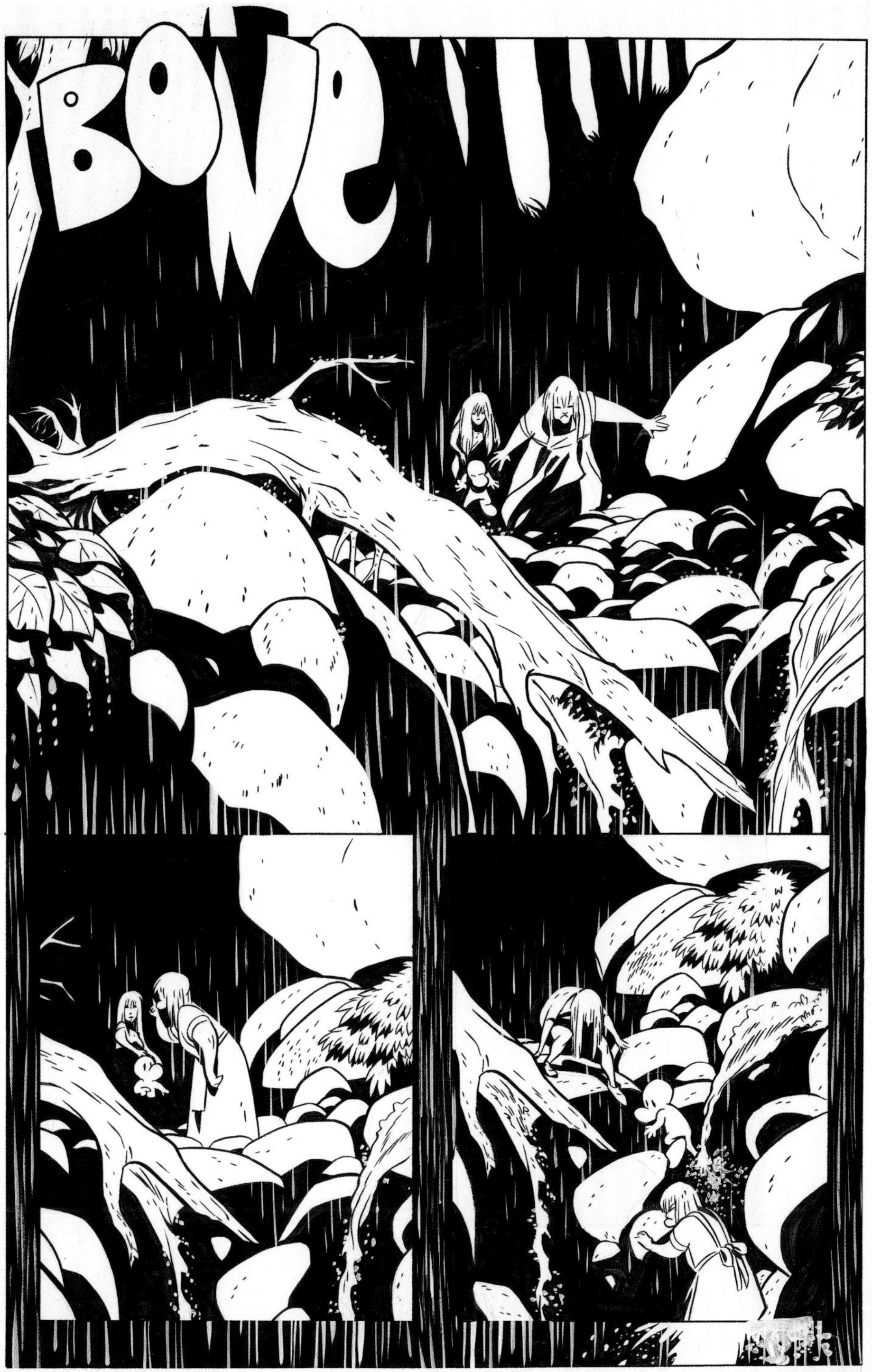
BONE

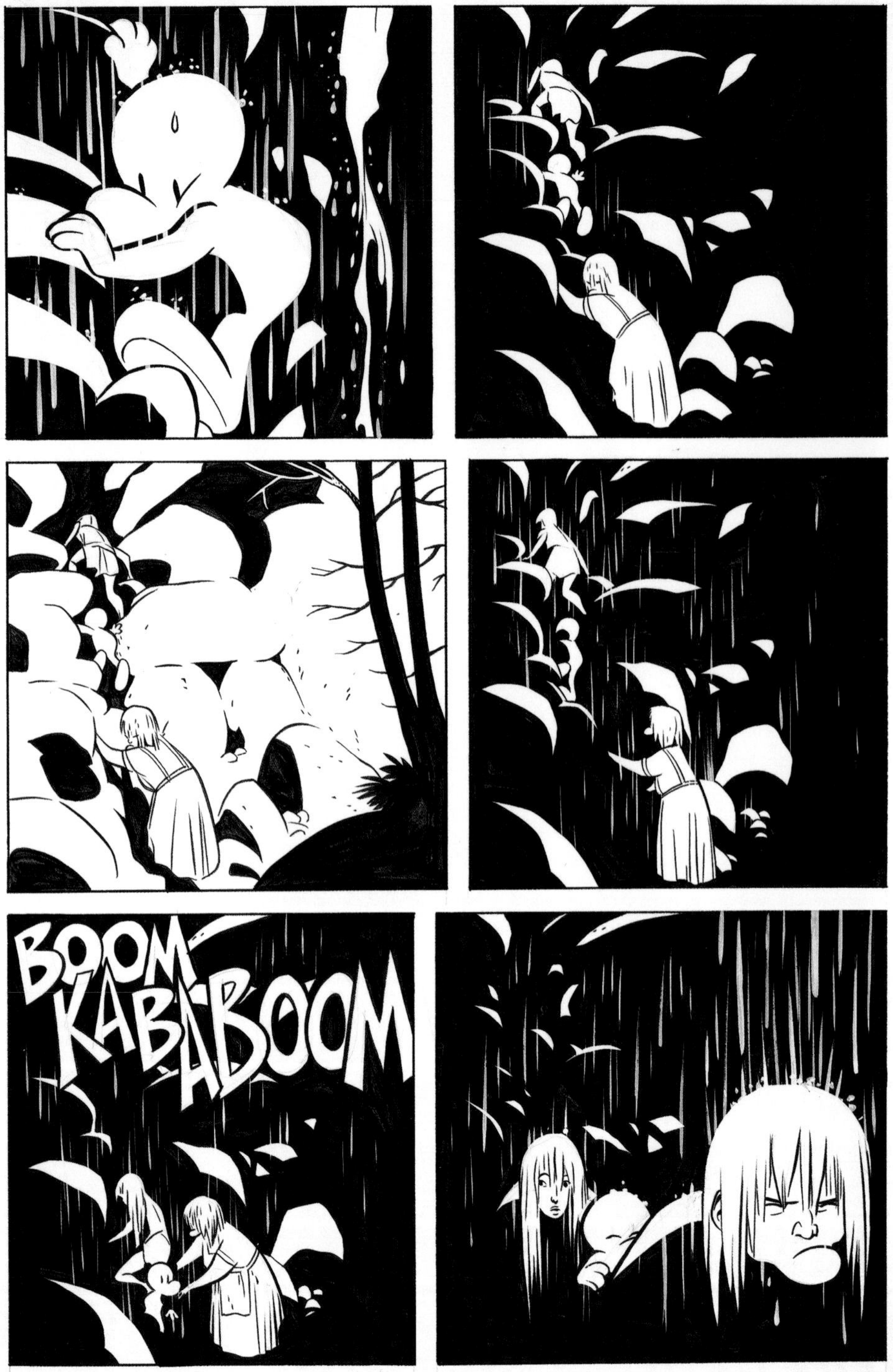
BOOM
KABABOOM

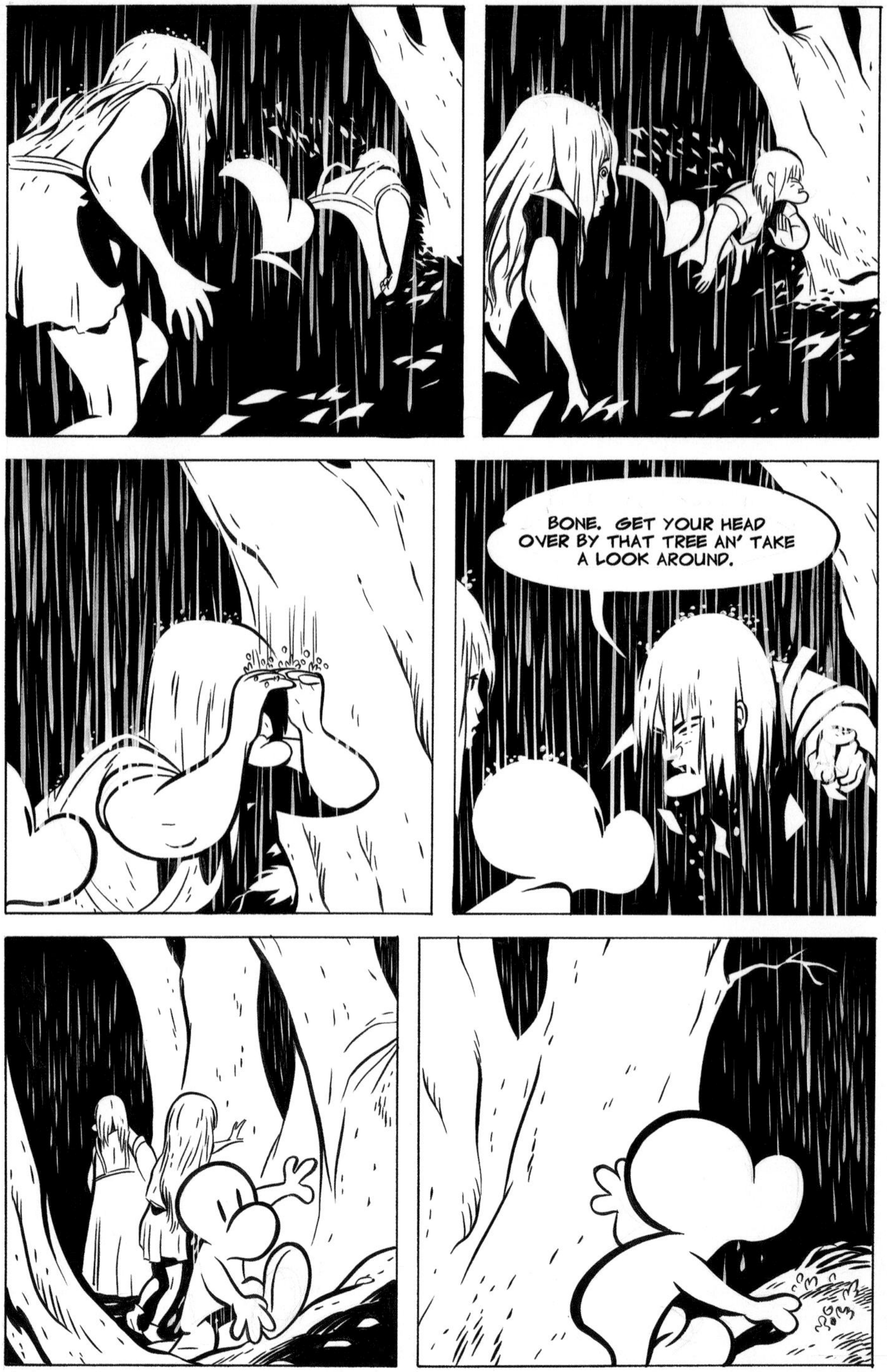
BONE. GET YOUR HEAD OVER BY THAT TREE AN' TAKE A LOOK AROUND.

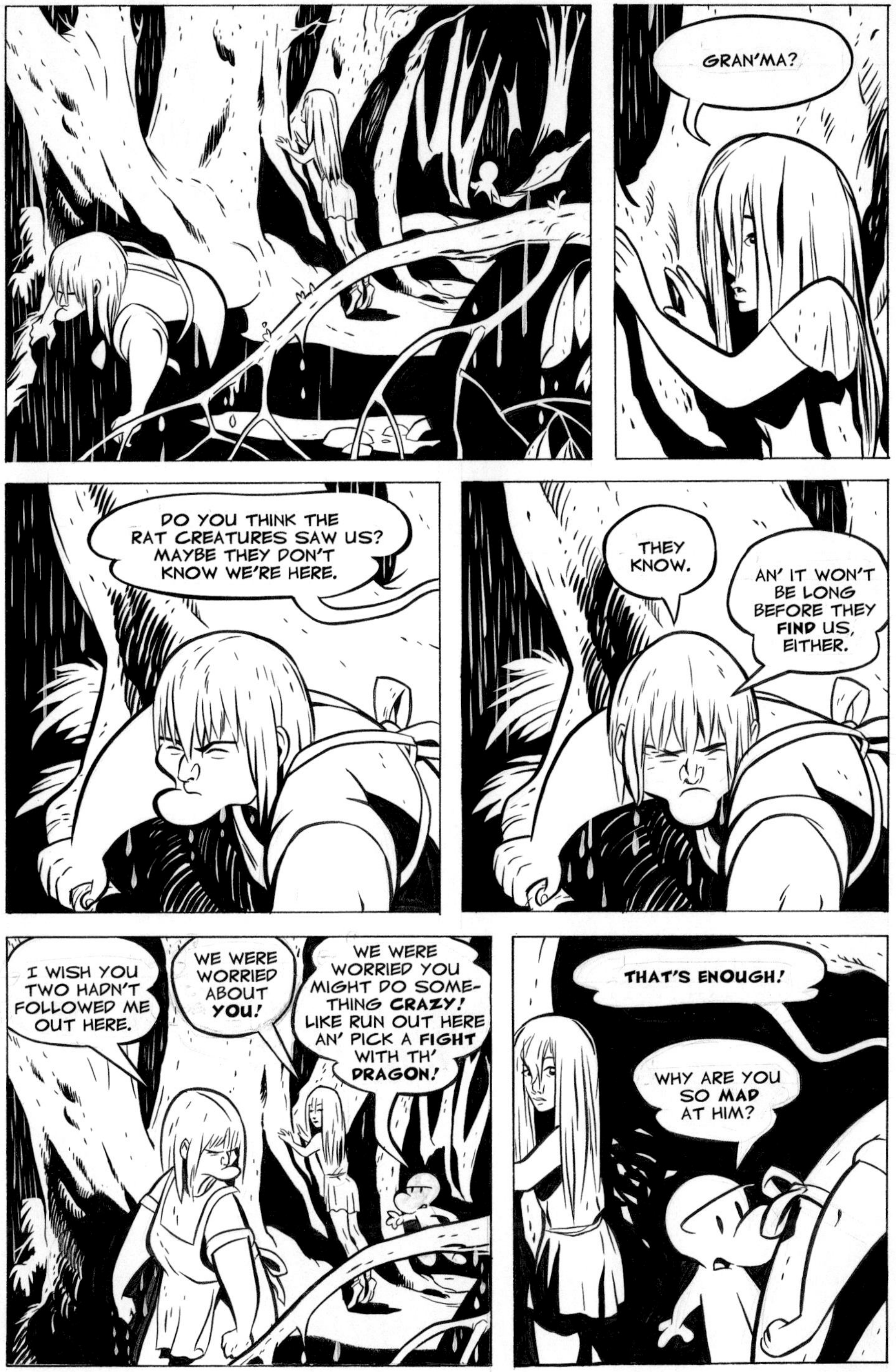
GRAN'MA?
DO YOU THINK THE RAT CREATURES SAW US? MAYBE THEY DON'T KNOW WE'RE HERE.
THEY KNOW.
AN' IT WON'T BE LONG BEFORE THEY **FIND** US, EITHER.
I WISH YOU TWO HADN'T FOLLOWED ME OUT HERE.
WE WERE WORRIED ABOUT **YOU!**
WE WERE WORRIED YOU MIGHT DO SOME-THING **CRAZY!** LIKE RUN OUT HERE AN' PICK A **FIGHT** WITH TH' **DRAGON!**
**THAT'S ENOUGH!**
WHY ARE YOU SO **MAD** AT HIM?

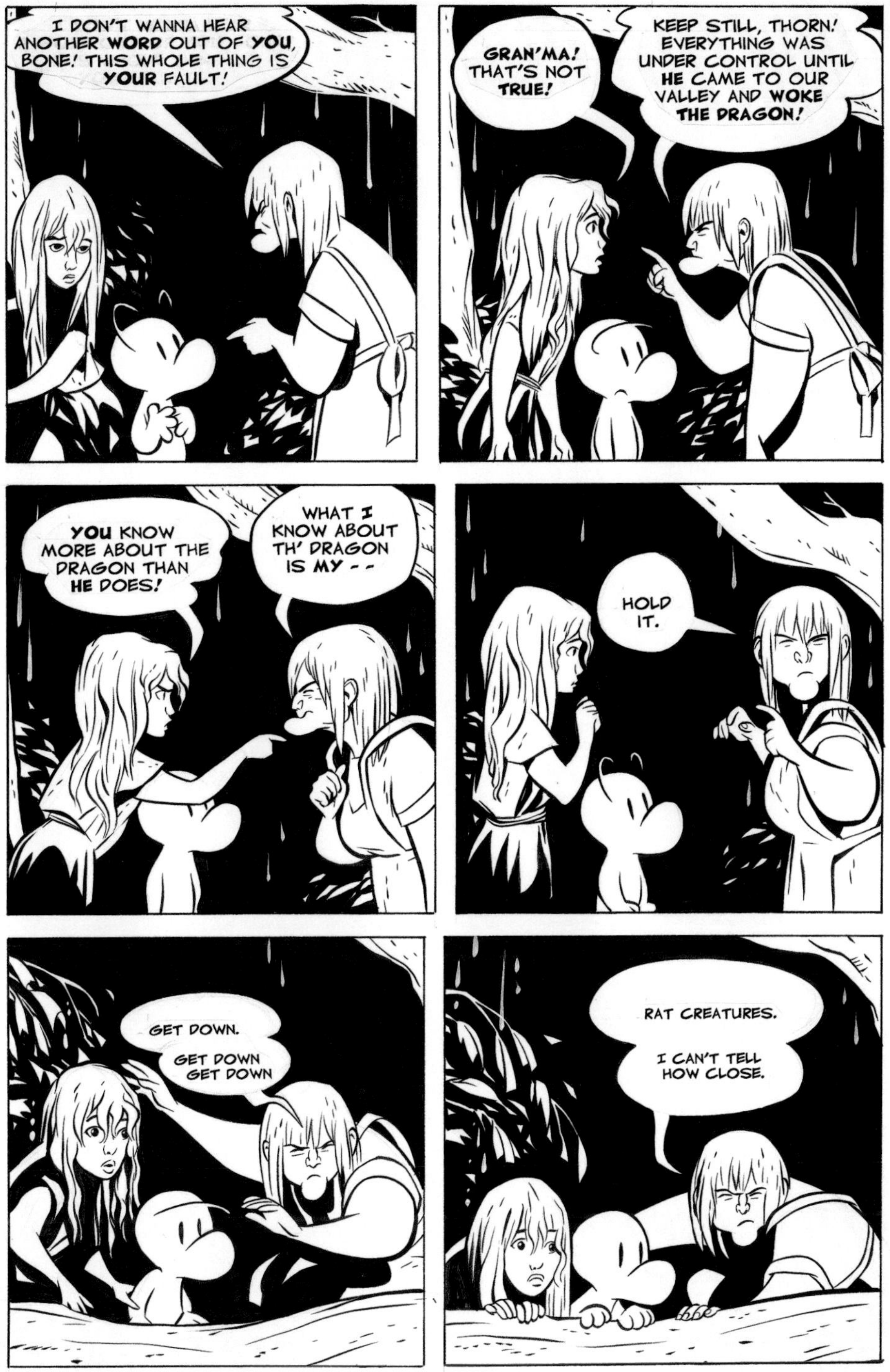
I DON'T WANNA HEAR ANOTHER **WORD** OUT OF **YOU**, BONE! THIS WHOLE THING IS **YOUR** FAULT!
**GRAN'MA!** THAT'S NOT **TRUE!**
KEEP STILL, THORN! EVERYTHING WAS UNDER CONTROL UNTIL **HE** CAME TO OUR VALLEY AND **WOKE THE DRAGON!**
**YOU** KNOW MORE ABOUT THE DRAGON THAN **HE** DOES!
WHAT **I** KNOW ABOUT TH' DRAGON IS **MY - -**
HOLD IT.
GET DOWN.
GET DOWN GET DOWN
RAT CREATURES.
I CAN'T TELL HOW CLOSE.

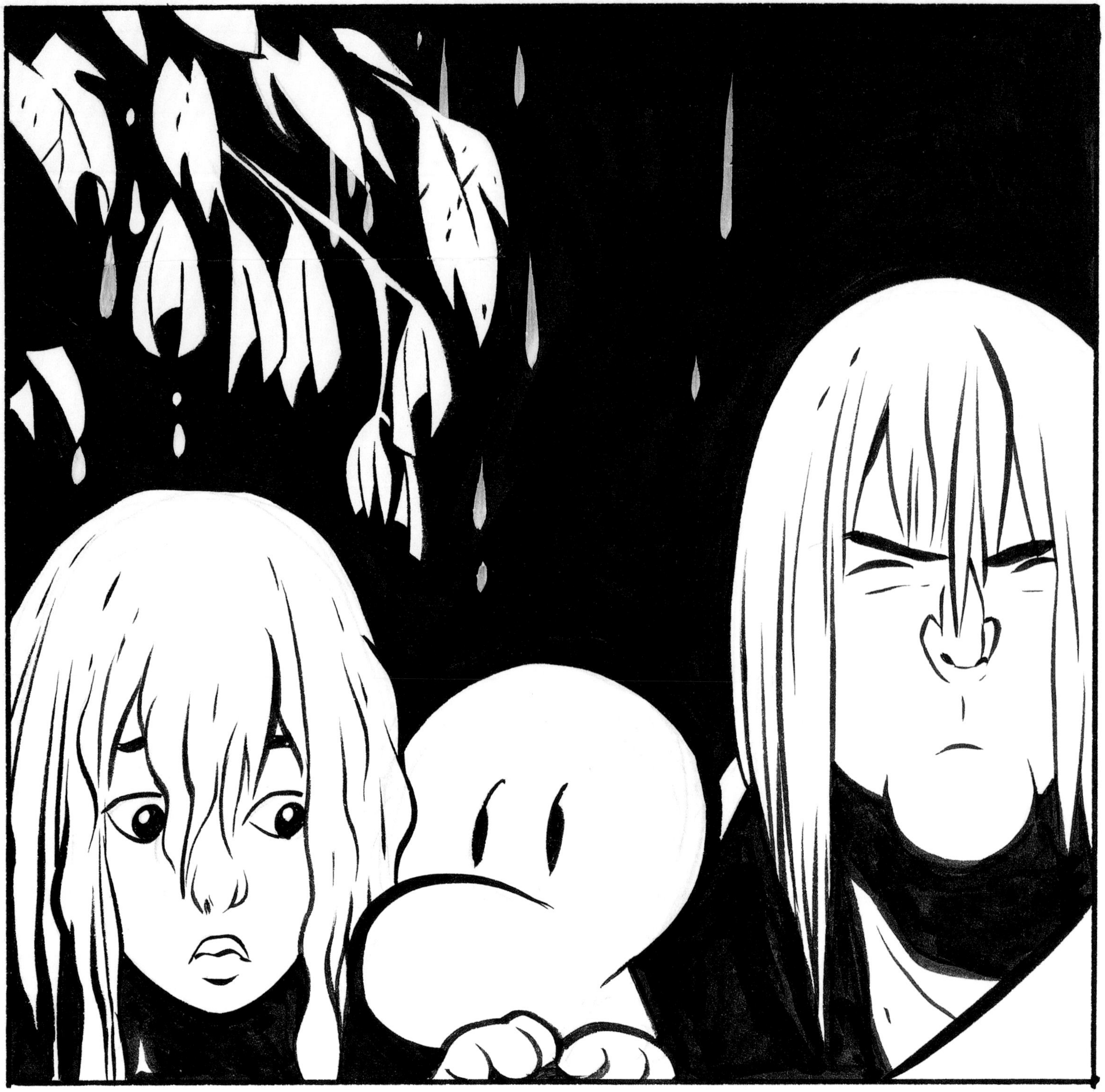

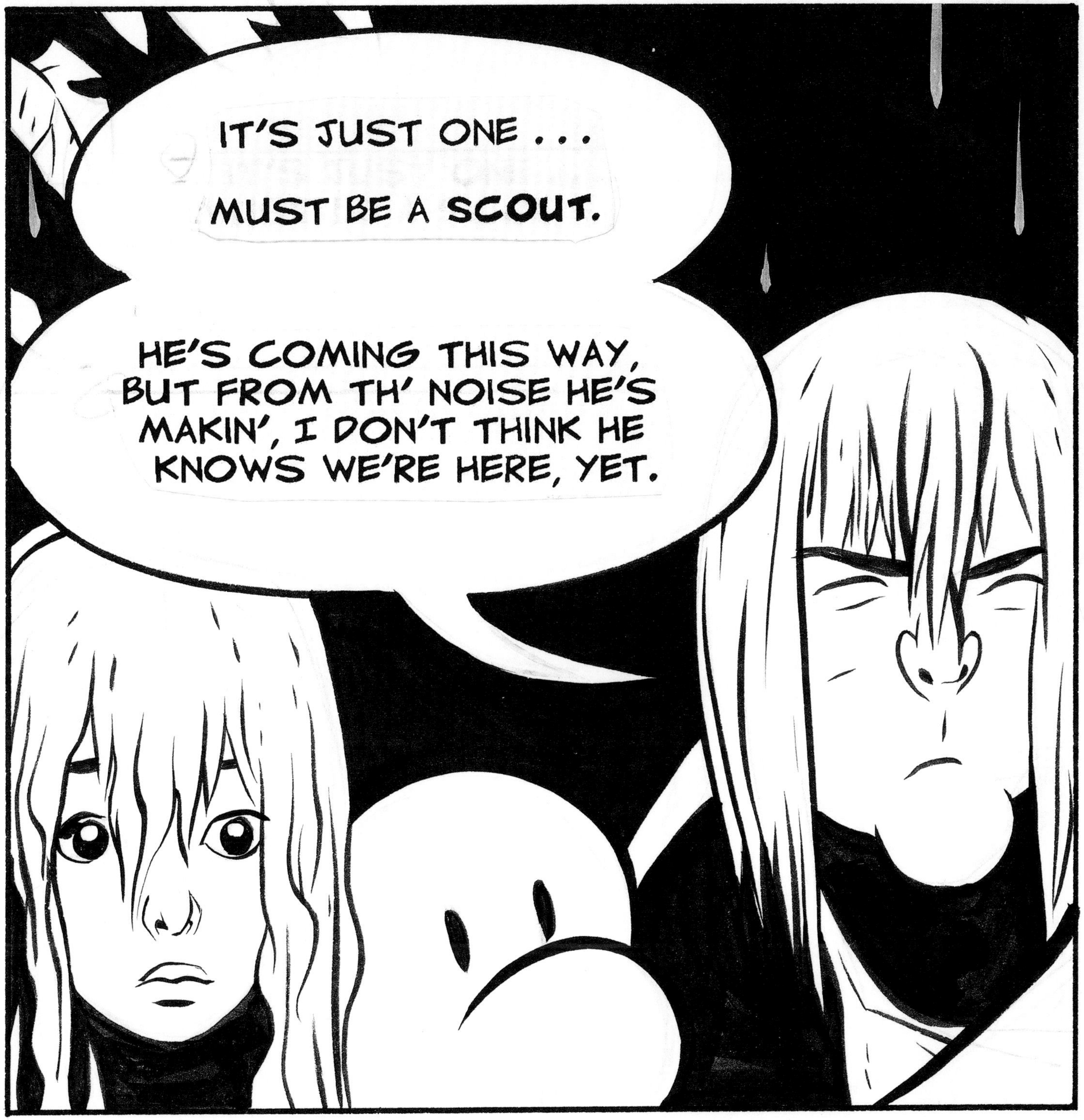
IT'S JUST ONE . . .
MUST BE A **SCOUT.**
HE'S COMING THIS WAY, BUT FROM TH' NOISE HE'S MAKIN', I DON'T THINK HE KNOWS WE'RE HERE, YET.

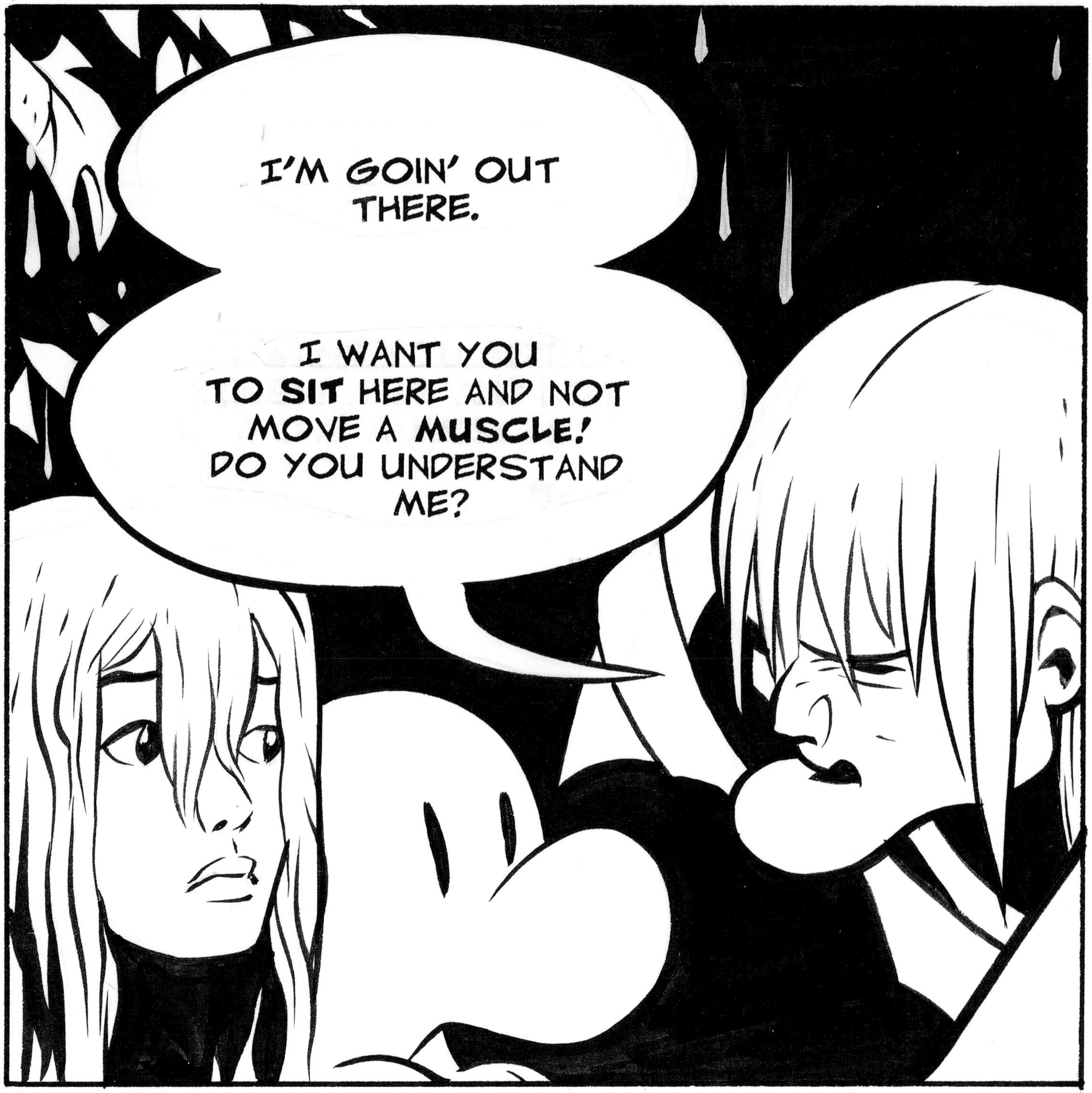
I'M GOIN' OUT THERE.
I WANT YOU TO SIT HERE AND NOT MOVE A MUSCLE! DO YOU UNDERSTAND ME?

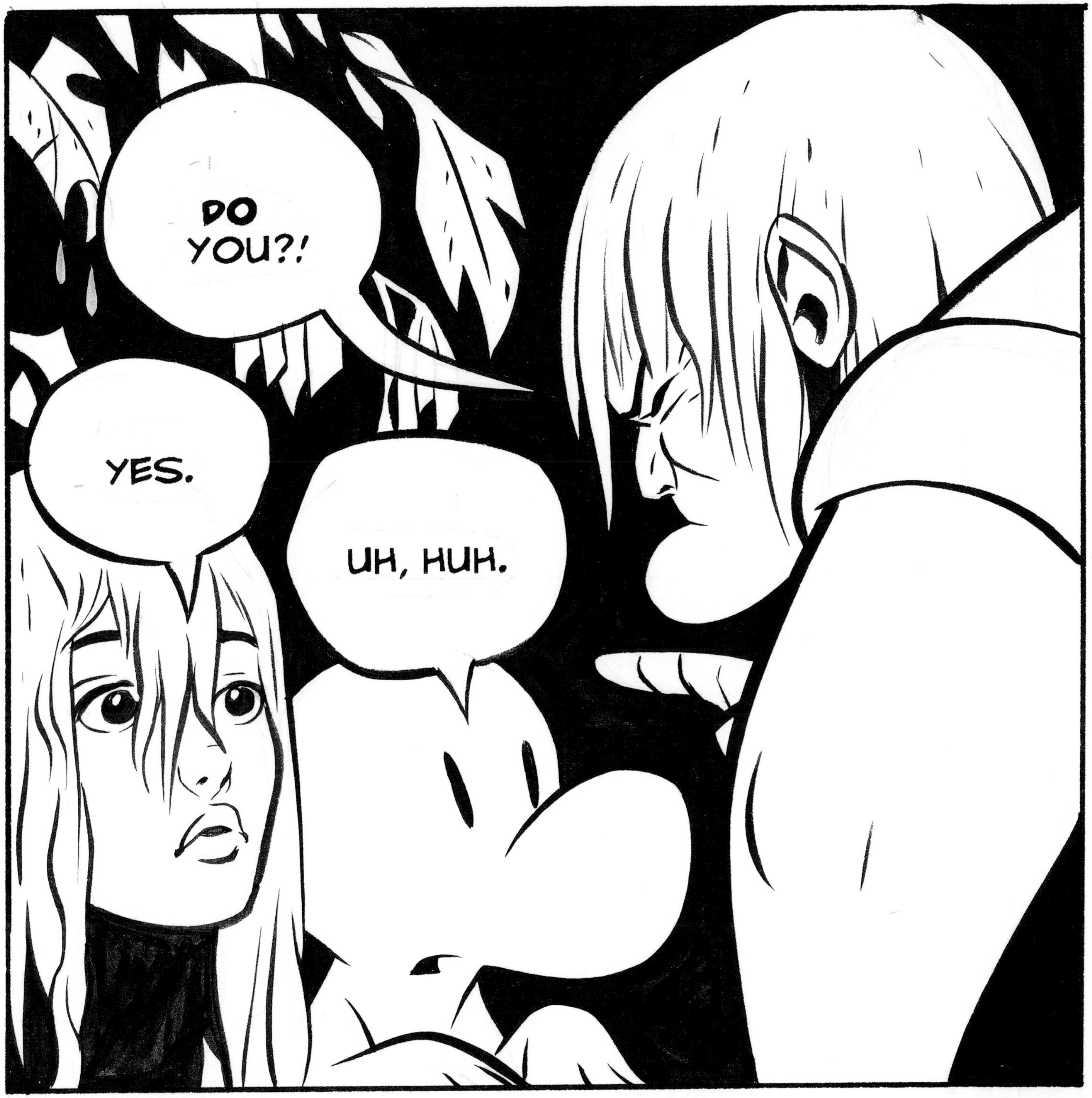
DO YOU?!
YES.
UH, HUH.

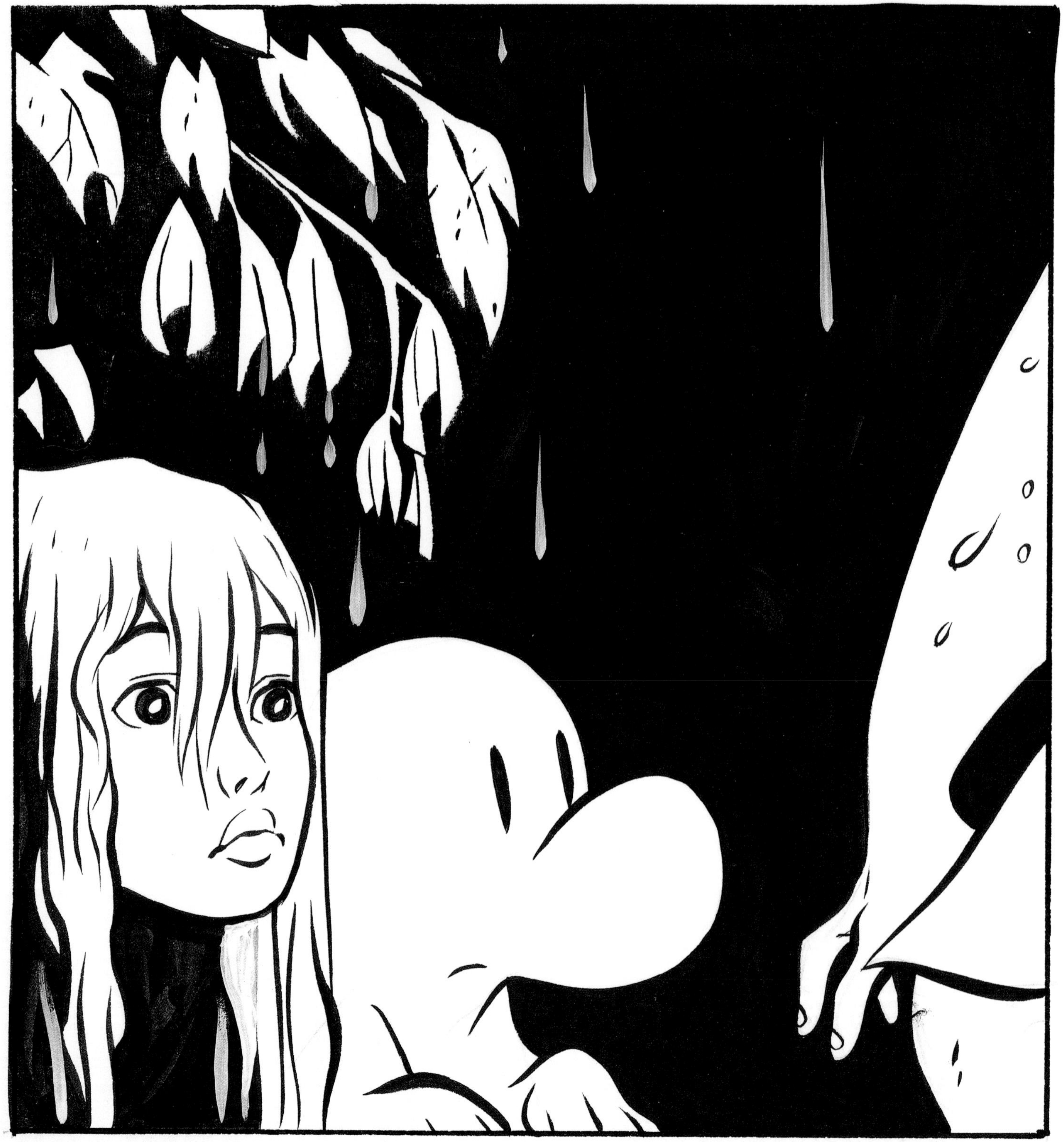

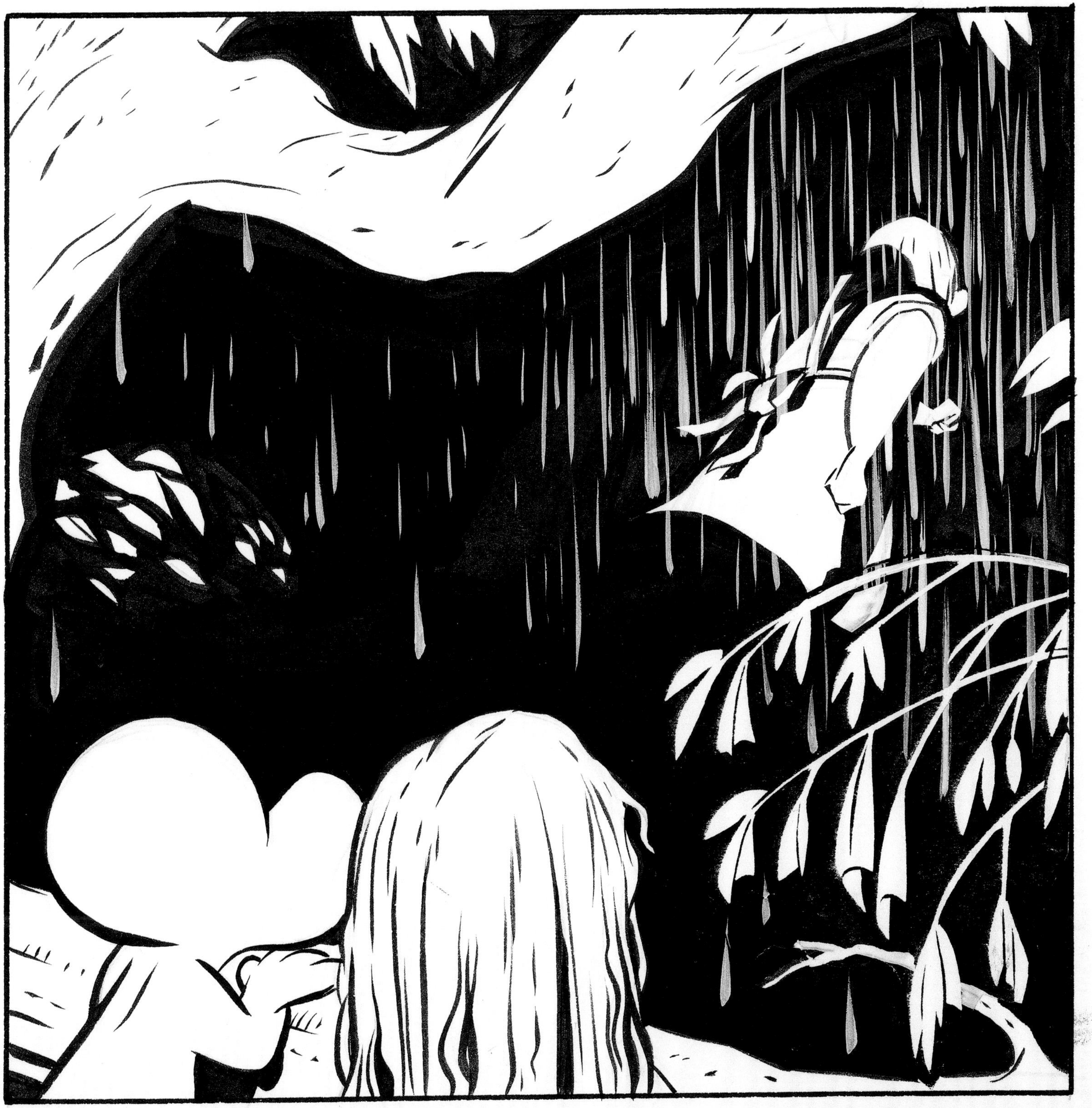

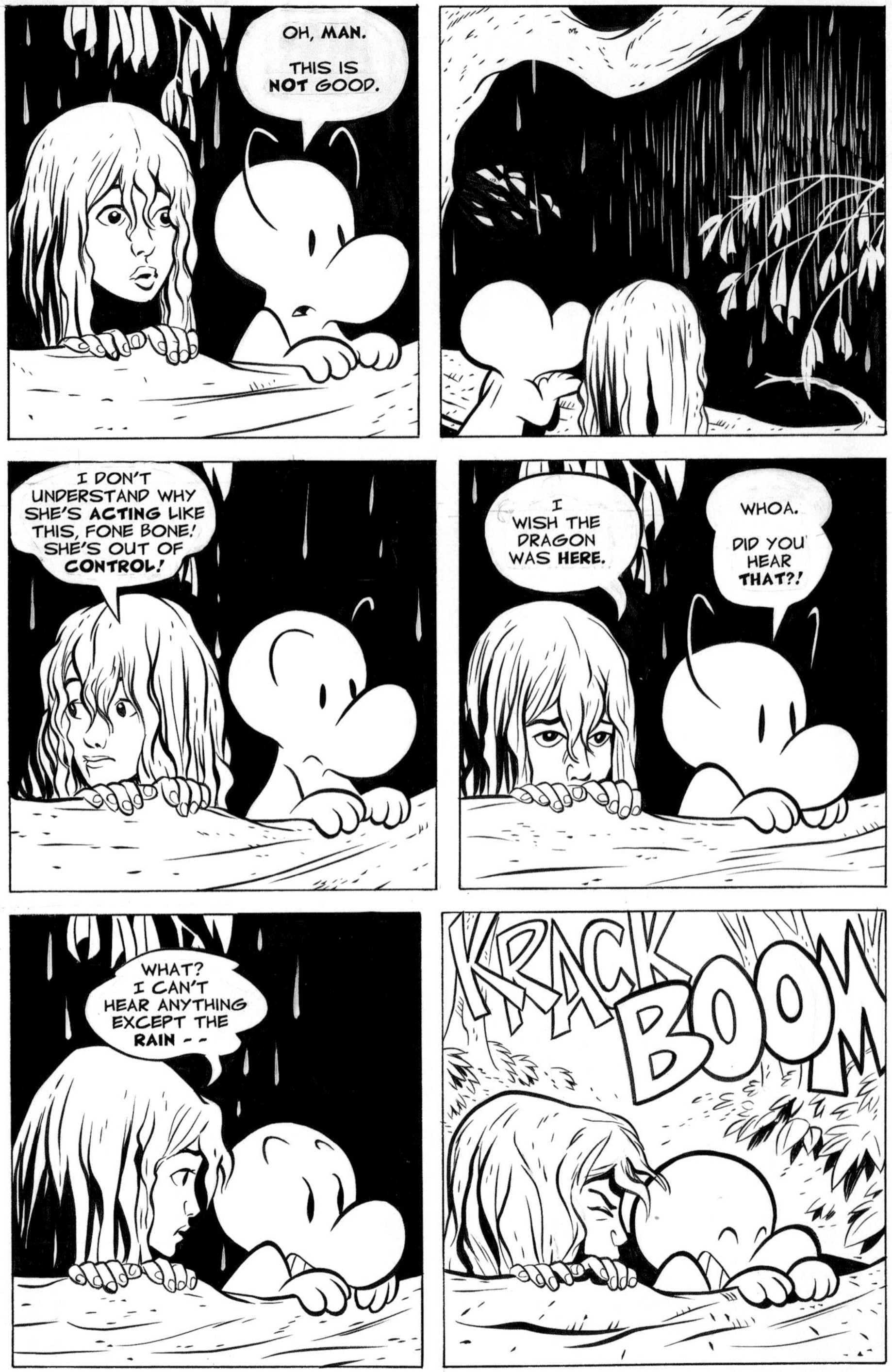
OH, MAN.
THIS IS NOT GOOD.
I DON'T UNDERSTAND WHY SHE'S ACTING LIKE THIS, FONE BONE! SHE'S OUT OF CONTROL!
I WISH THE DRAGON WAS HERE.
WHOA.
DID YOU HEAR THAT?!
WHAT? I CAN'T HEAR ANYTHING EXCEPT THE RAIN --
KRACK
BOOOM

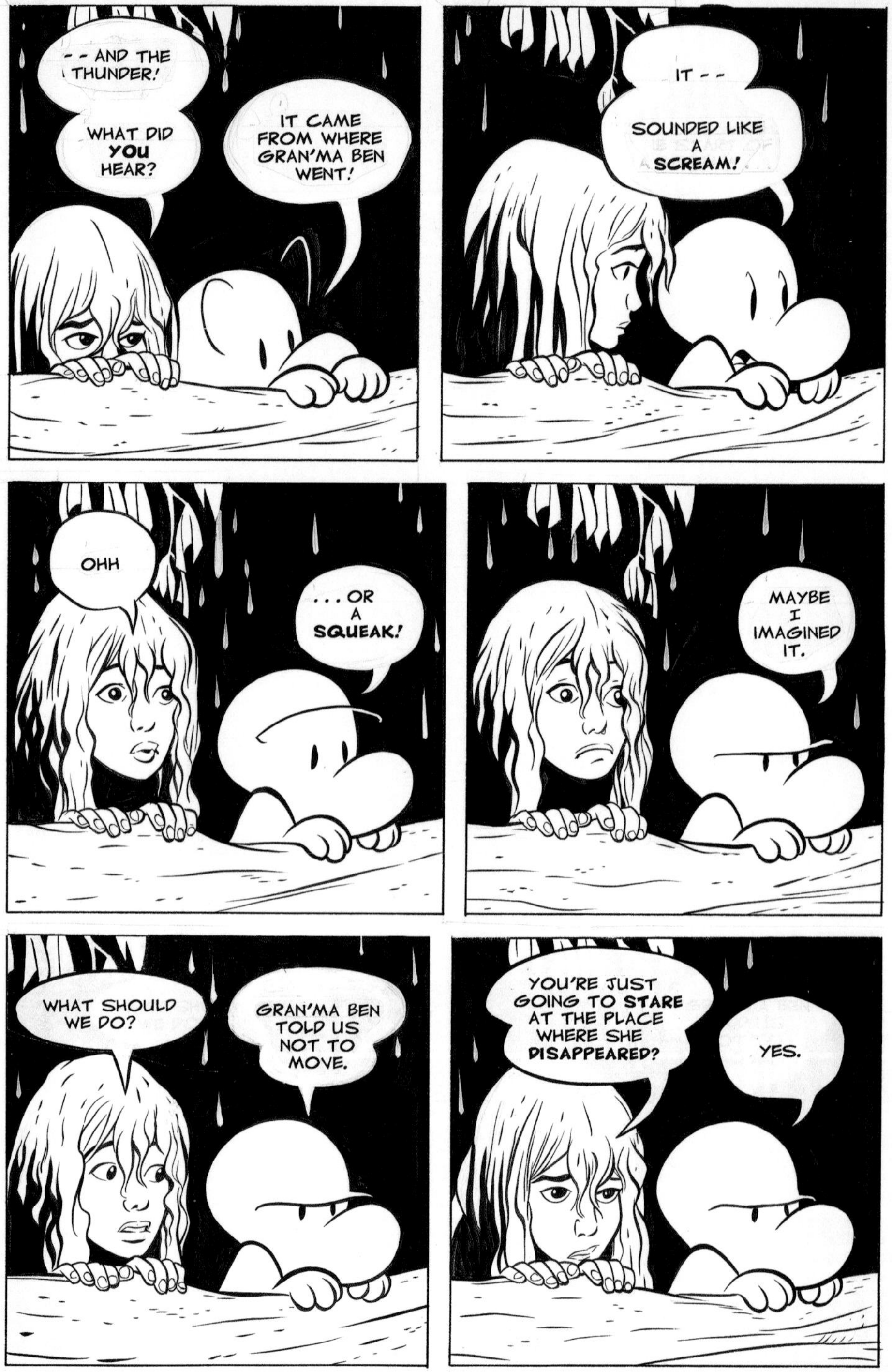
-- AND THE THUNDER!
WHAT DID YOU HEAR?
IT CAME FROM WHERE GRAN'MA BEN WENT!
IT --
SOUNDED LIKE A SCREAM!
OHH
...OR A SQUEAK!
MAYBE I IMAGINED IT.
WHAT SHOULD WE DO?
GRAN'MA BEN TOLD US NOT TO MOVE.
YOU'RE JUST GOING TO STARE AT THE PLACE WHERE SHE DISAPPEARED?
YES.

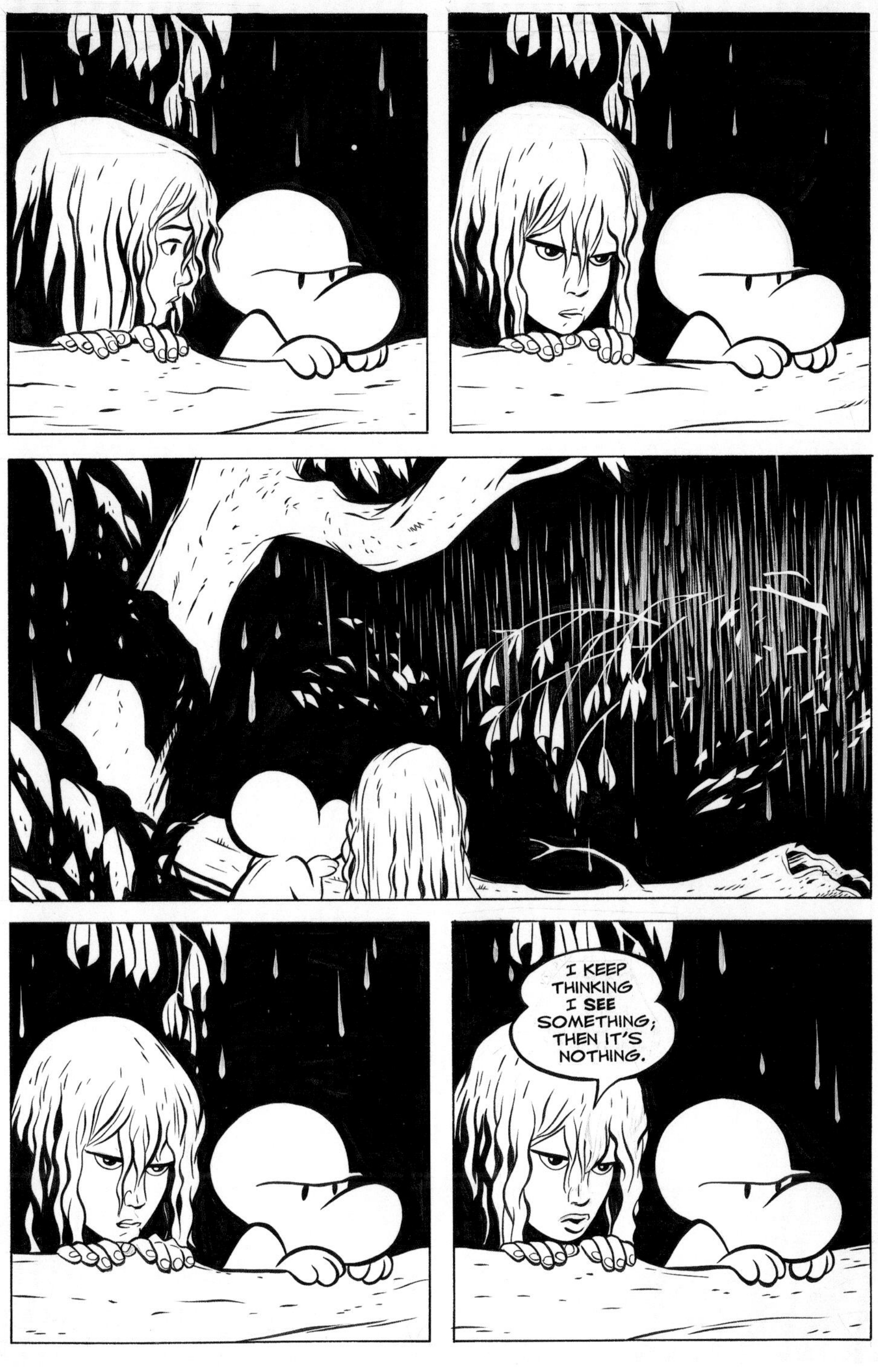
I KEEP THINKING I **SEE** SOMETHING; THEN IT'S NOTHING.

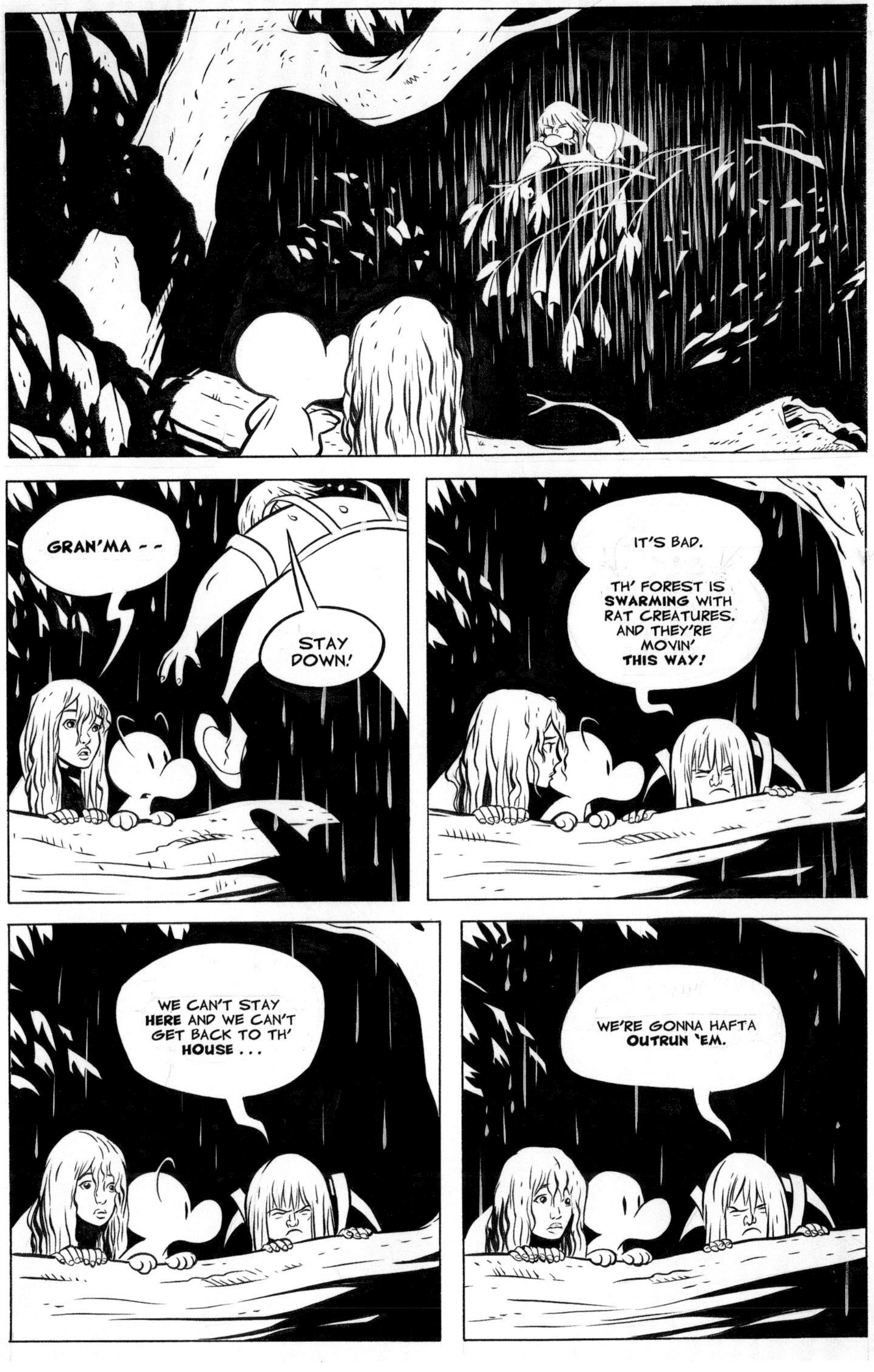
GRAN'MA - -
STAY DOWN!
IT'S BAD. TH' FOREST IS **SWARMING** WITH RAT CREATURES. AND THEY'RE MOVIN' **THIS WAY!**
WE CAN'T STAY **HERE** AND WE CAN'T GET BACK TO TH' **HOUSE** . . .
WE'RE GONNA HAFTA **OUTRUN** 'EM.

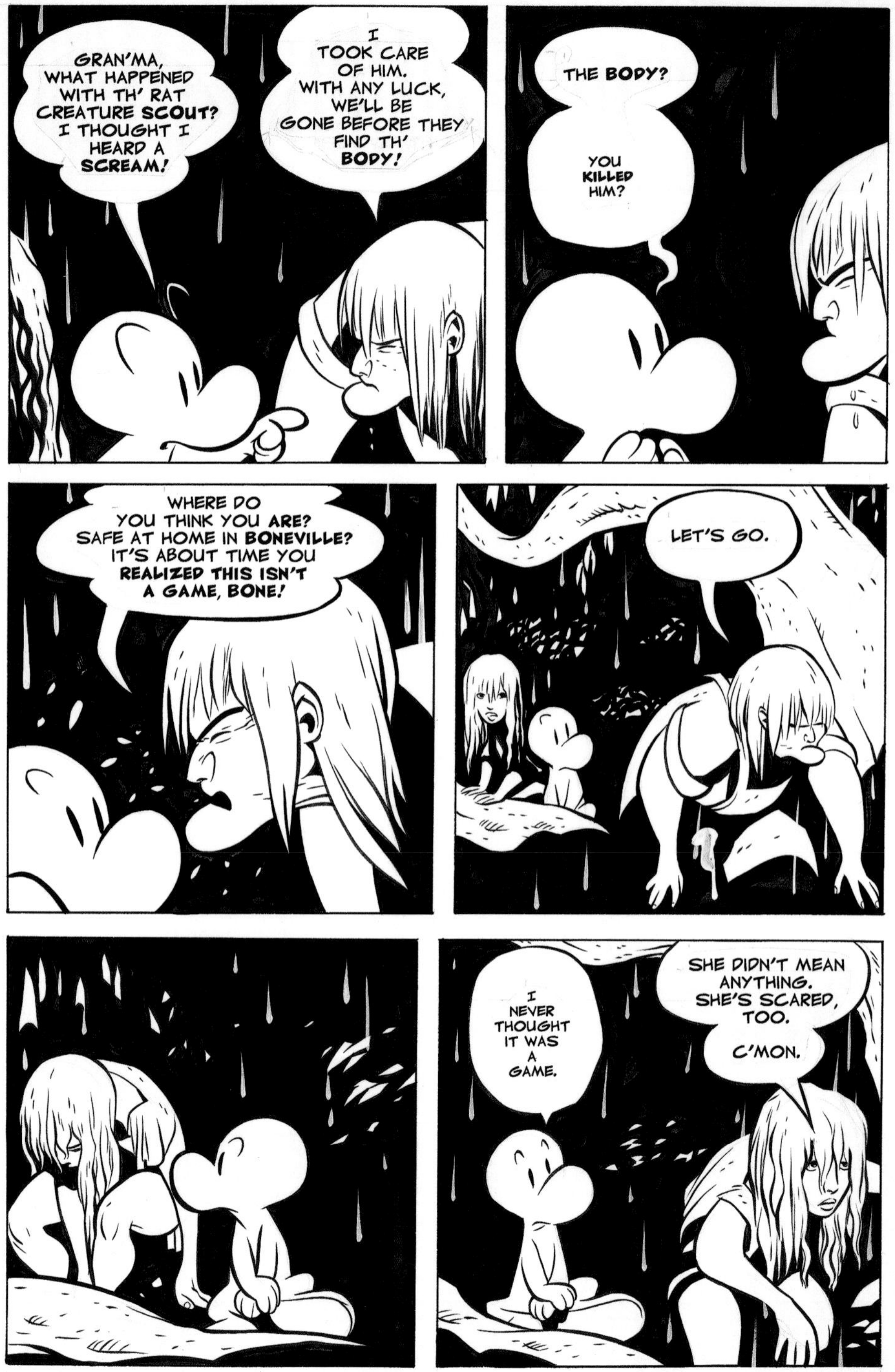
GRAN'MA, WHAT HAPPENED WITH TH' RAT CREATURE **SCOUT?** I THOUGHT I HEARD A **SCREAM!**
I TOOK CARE OF HIM. WITH ANY LUCK, WE'LL BE GONE BEFORE THEY FIND TH' **BODY!**
THE **BODY?**
YOU **KILLED** HIM?
WHERE DO YOU THINK YOU **ARE?** SAFE AT HOME IN **BONEVILLE?** IT'S ABOUT TIME YOU **REALIZED THIS ISN'T A GAME, BONE!**
LET'S GO.
I NEVER THOUGHT IT WAS A GAME.
SHE DIDN'T MEAN ANYTHING. SHE'S SCARED, TOO.
C'MON.

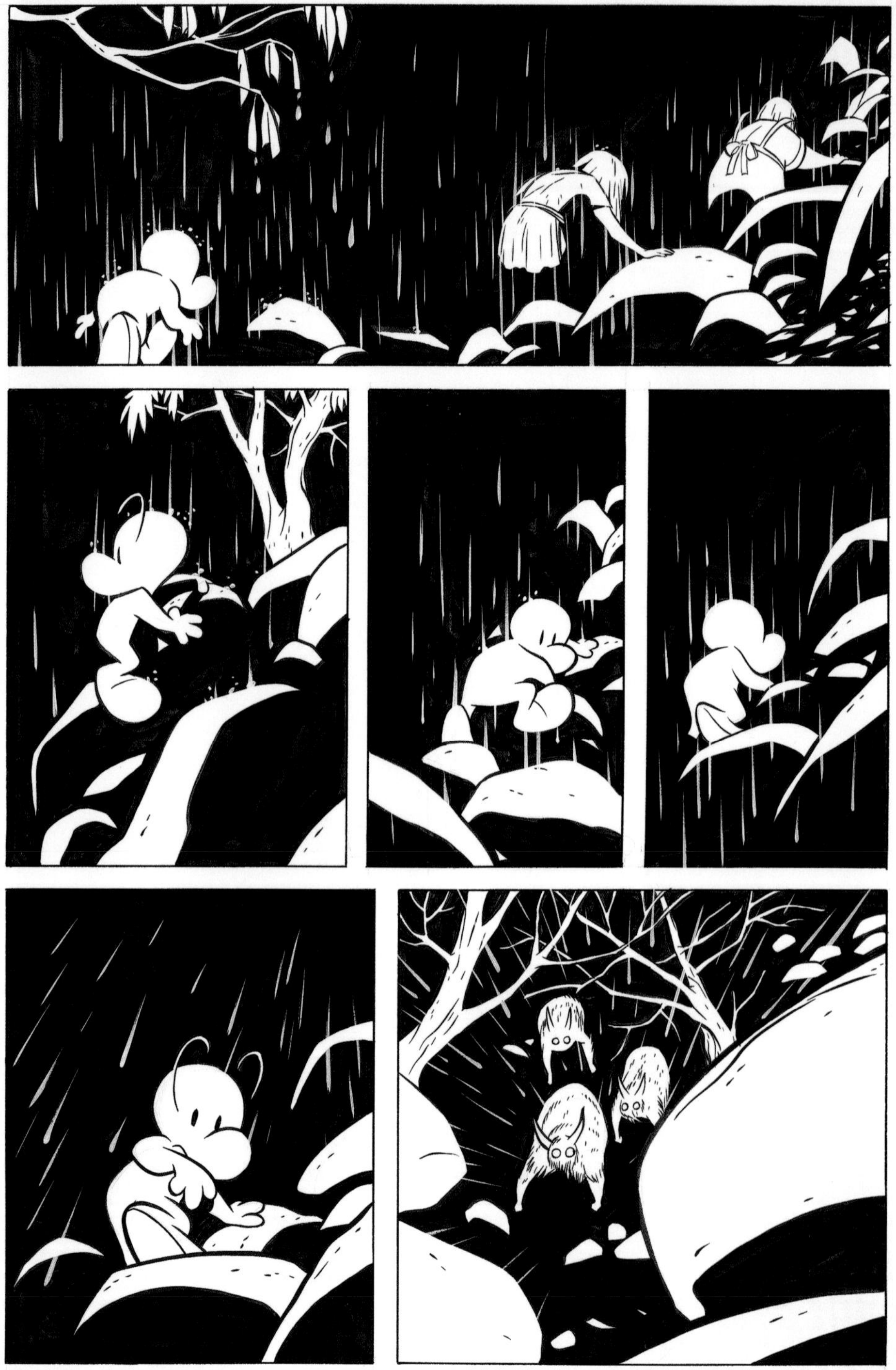

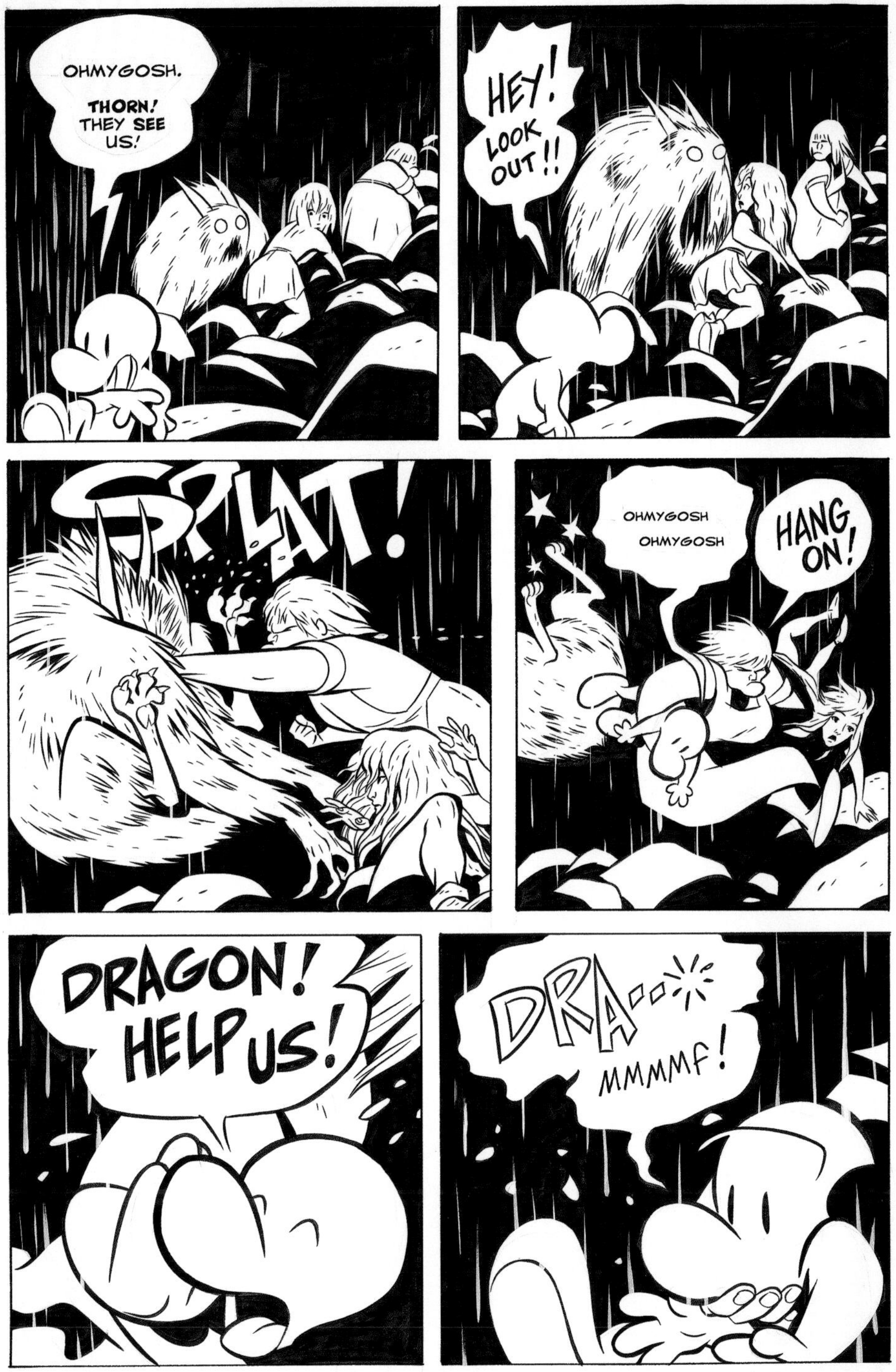
OHMYGOSH.
THORN! THEY SEE US!
HEY! LOOK OUT!!
SPLAT!
OHMYGOSH OHMYGOSH
HANG ON!
DRAGON! HELP US!
DRA--
MMMMF!

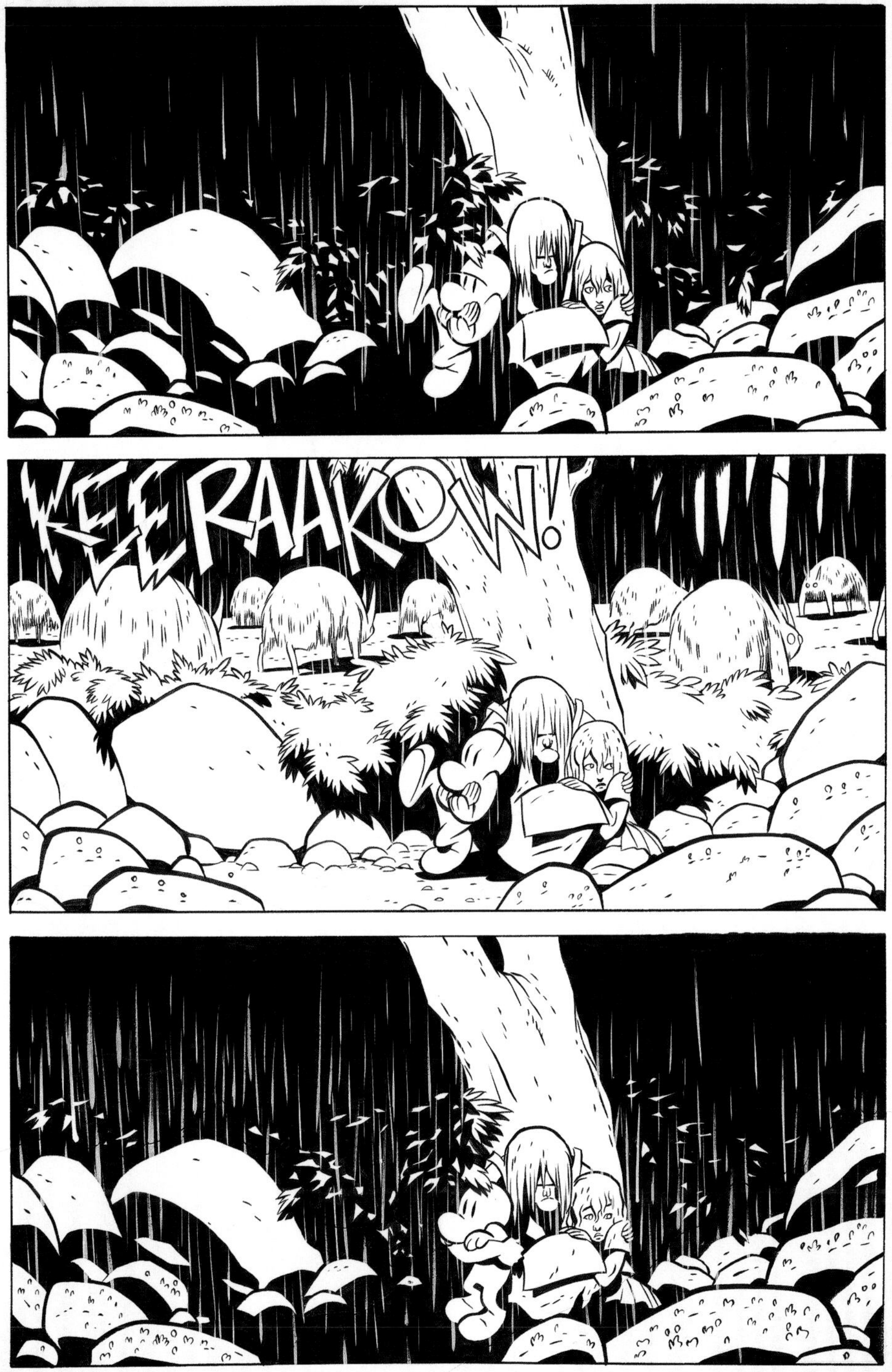
KEERAAKOW!

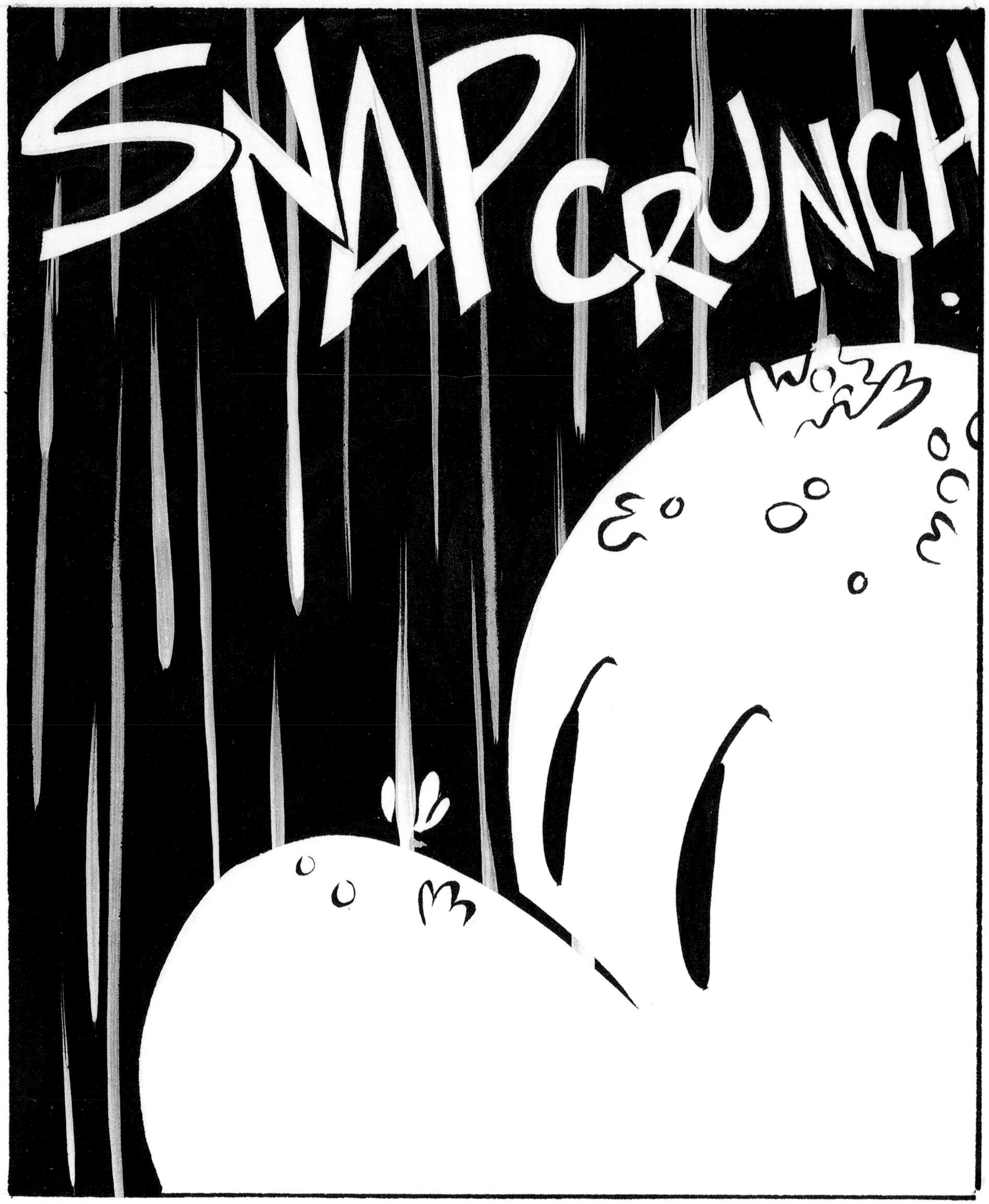
SNAP
CRUNCH

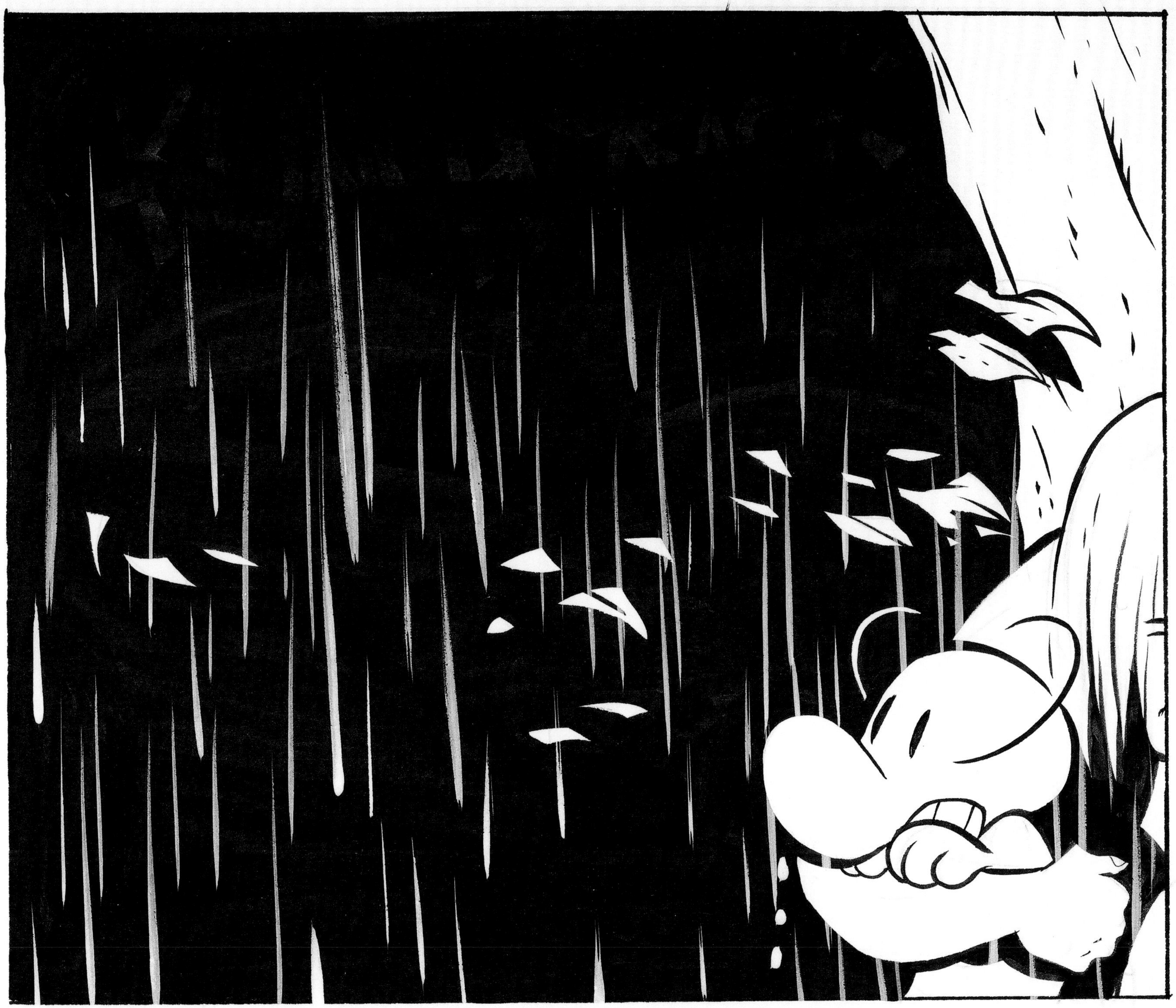

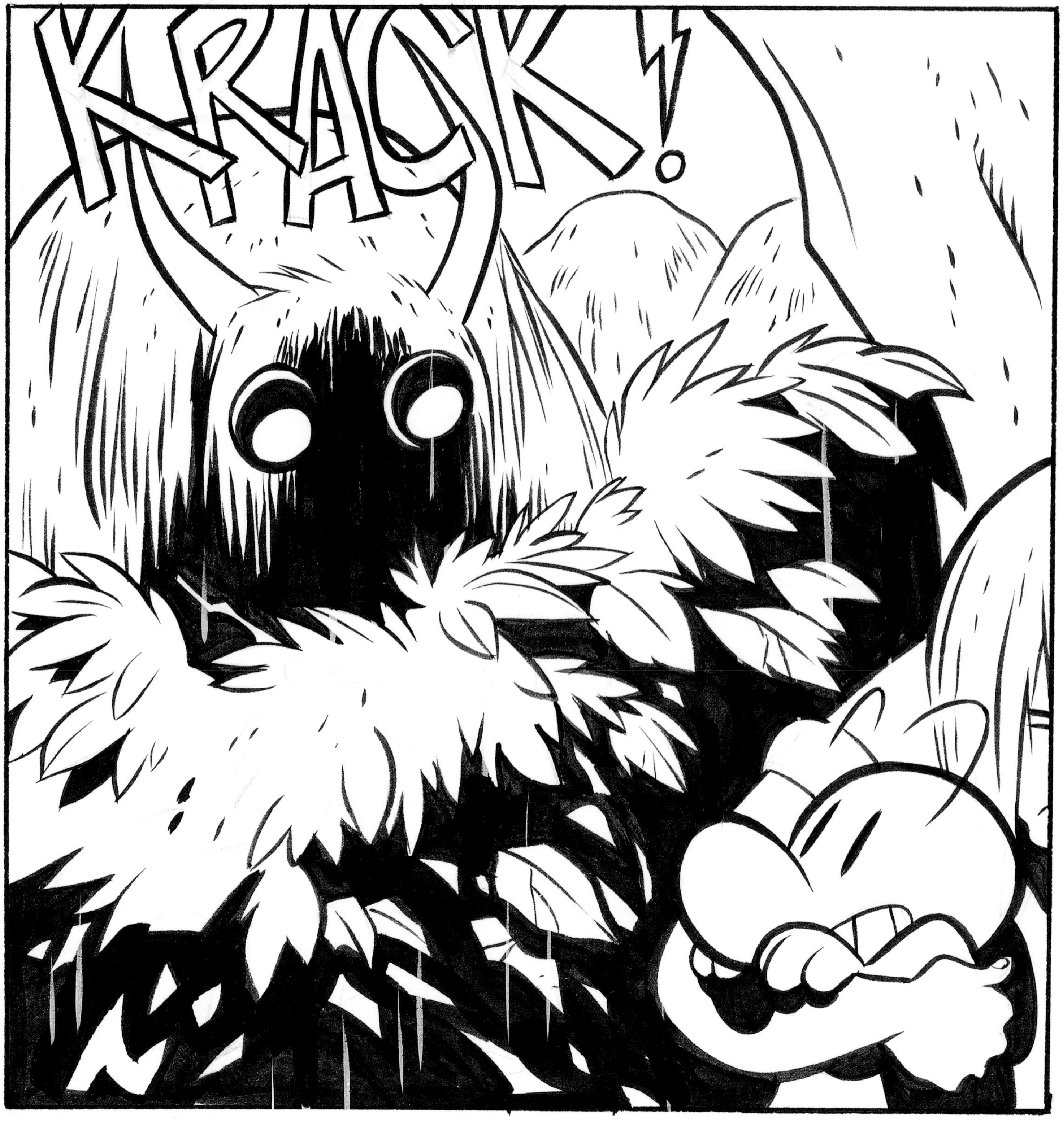
KRACK!

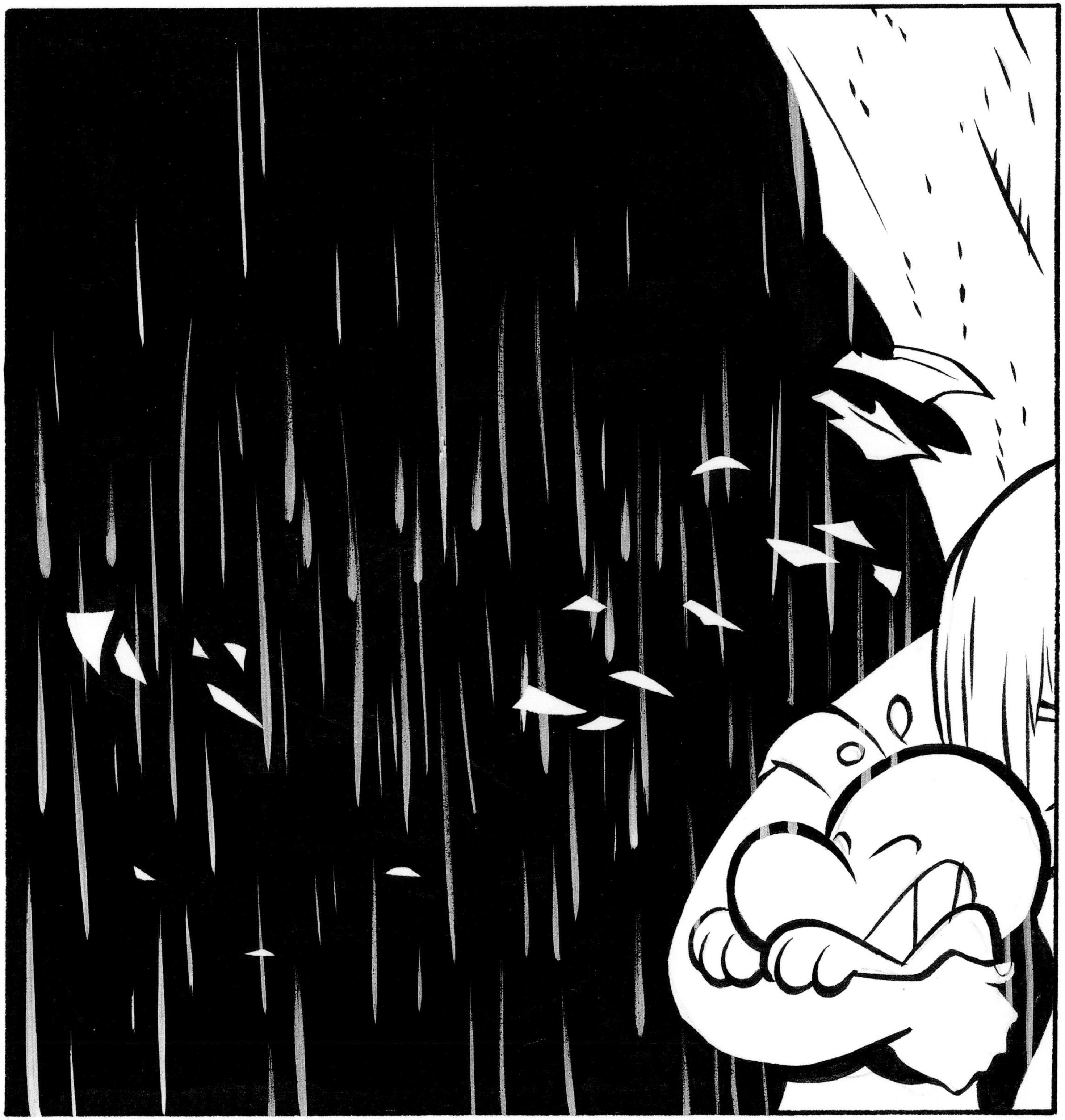

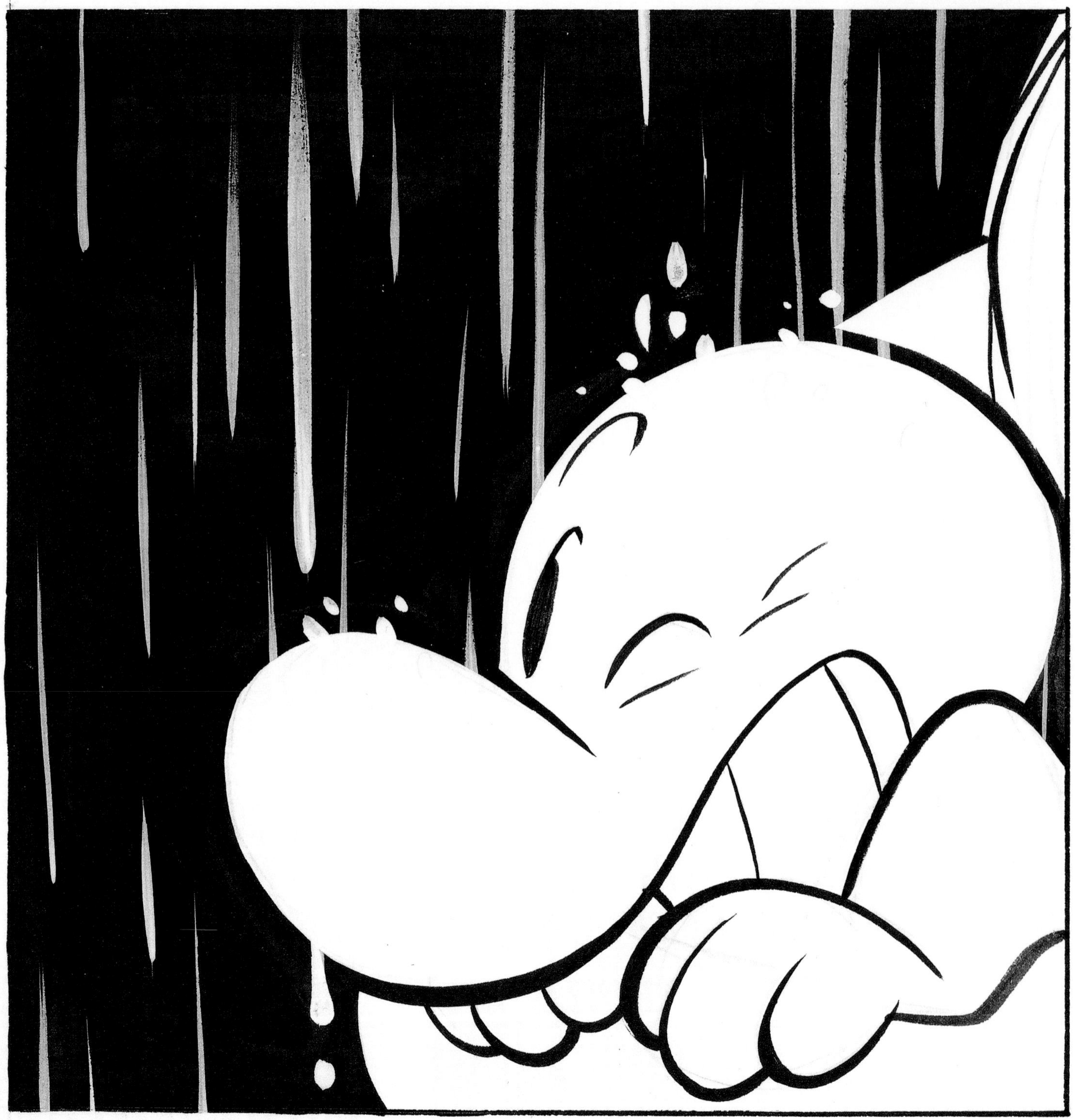

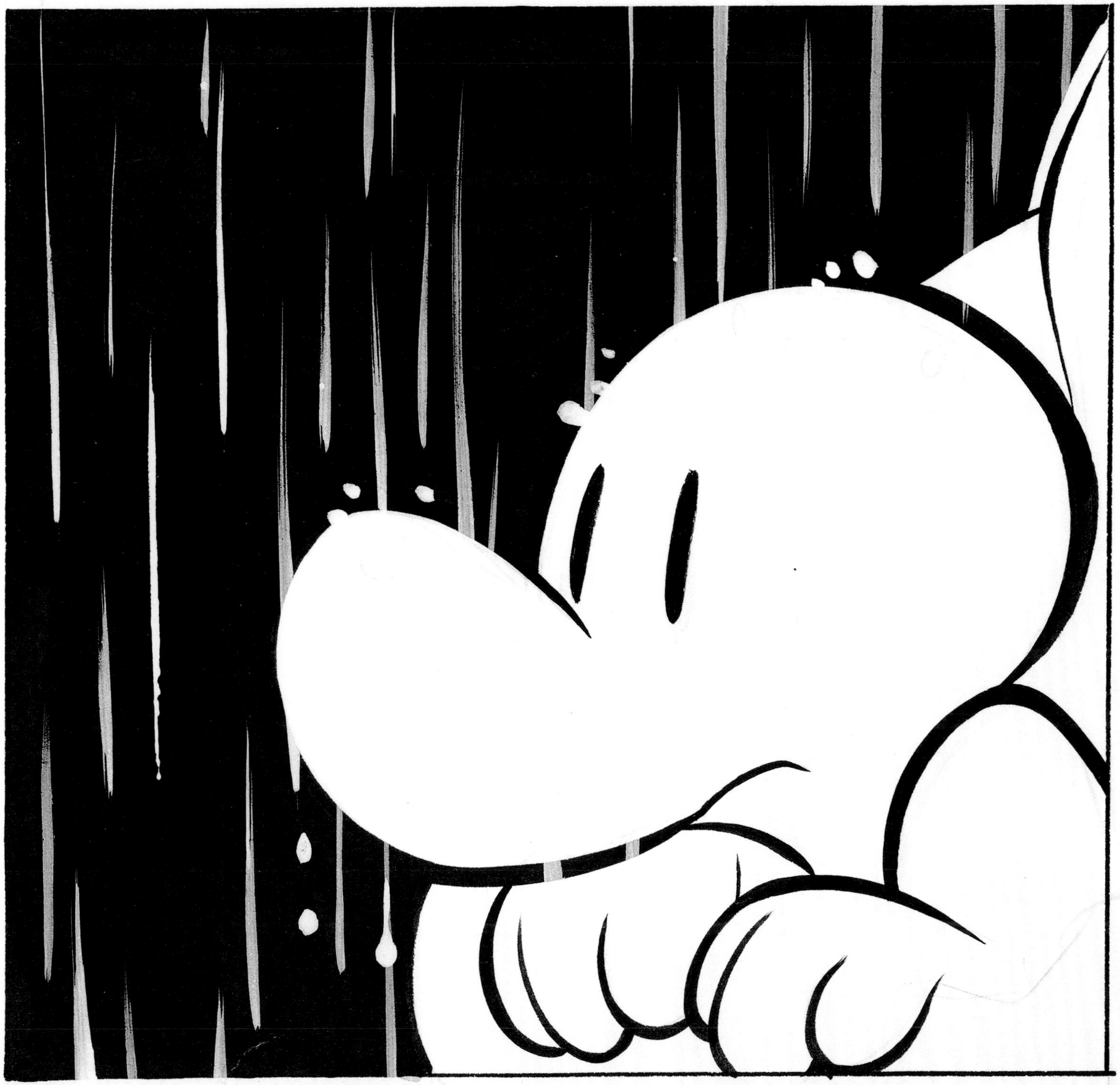

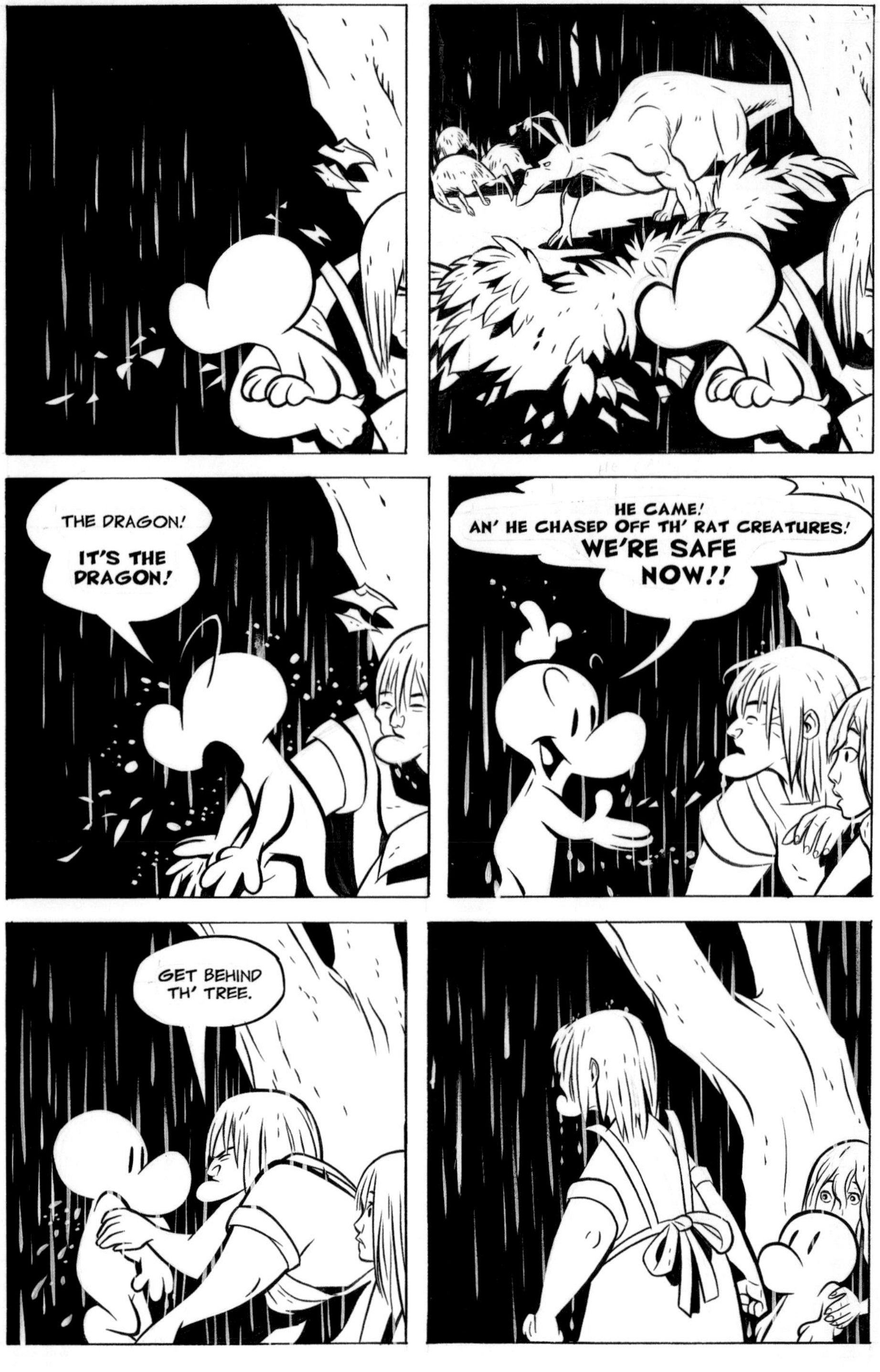
THE DRAGON! IT'S THE DRAGON!
HE CAME! AN' HE CHASED OFF TH' RAT CREATURES! WE'RE SAFE NOW!!
GET BEHIND TH' TREE.

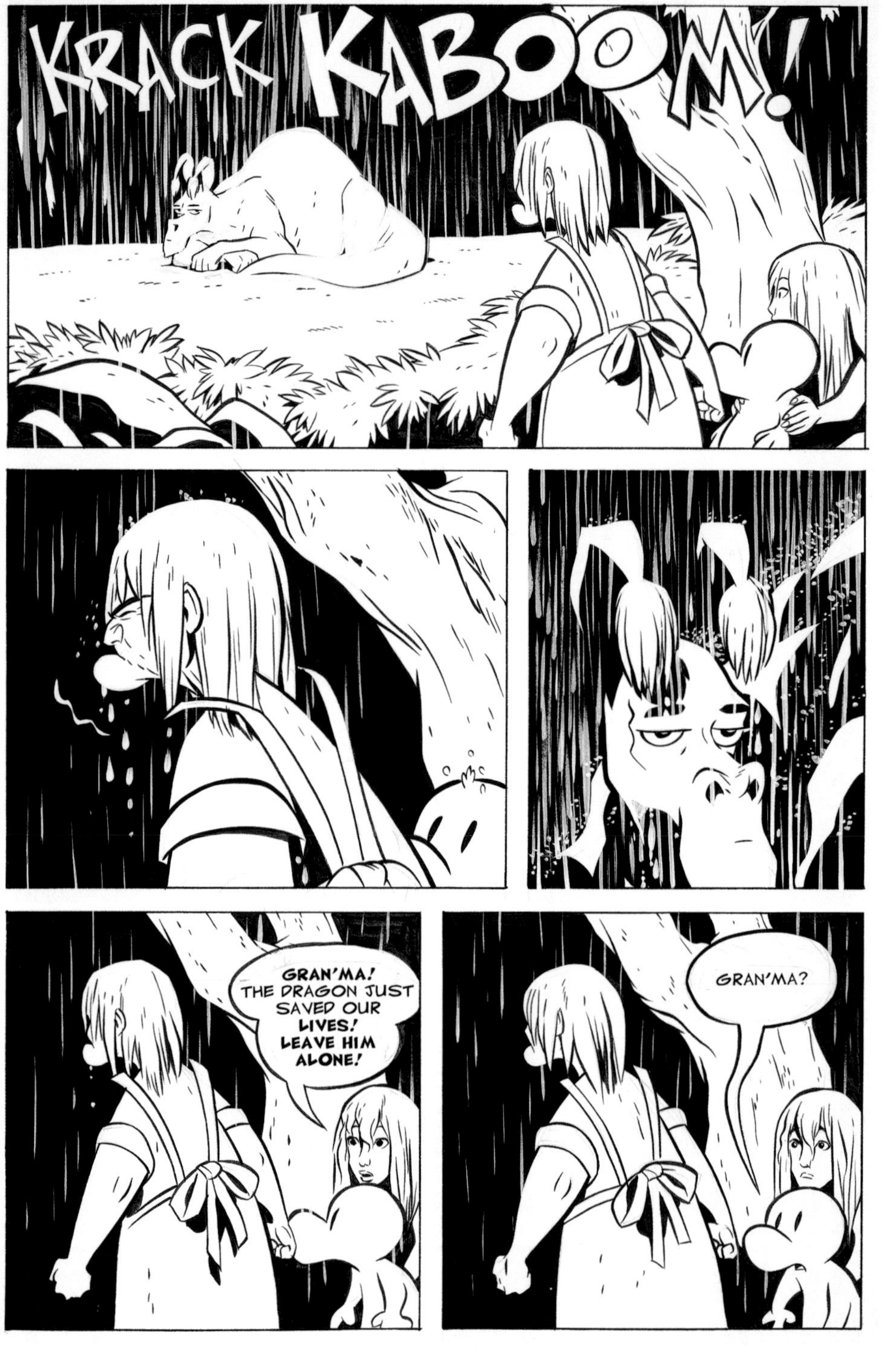
KRACK KABOOM!
GRAN'MA! THE DRAGON JUST SAVED OUR LIVES! LEAVE HIM ALONE!
GRAN'MA?

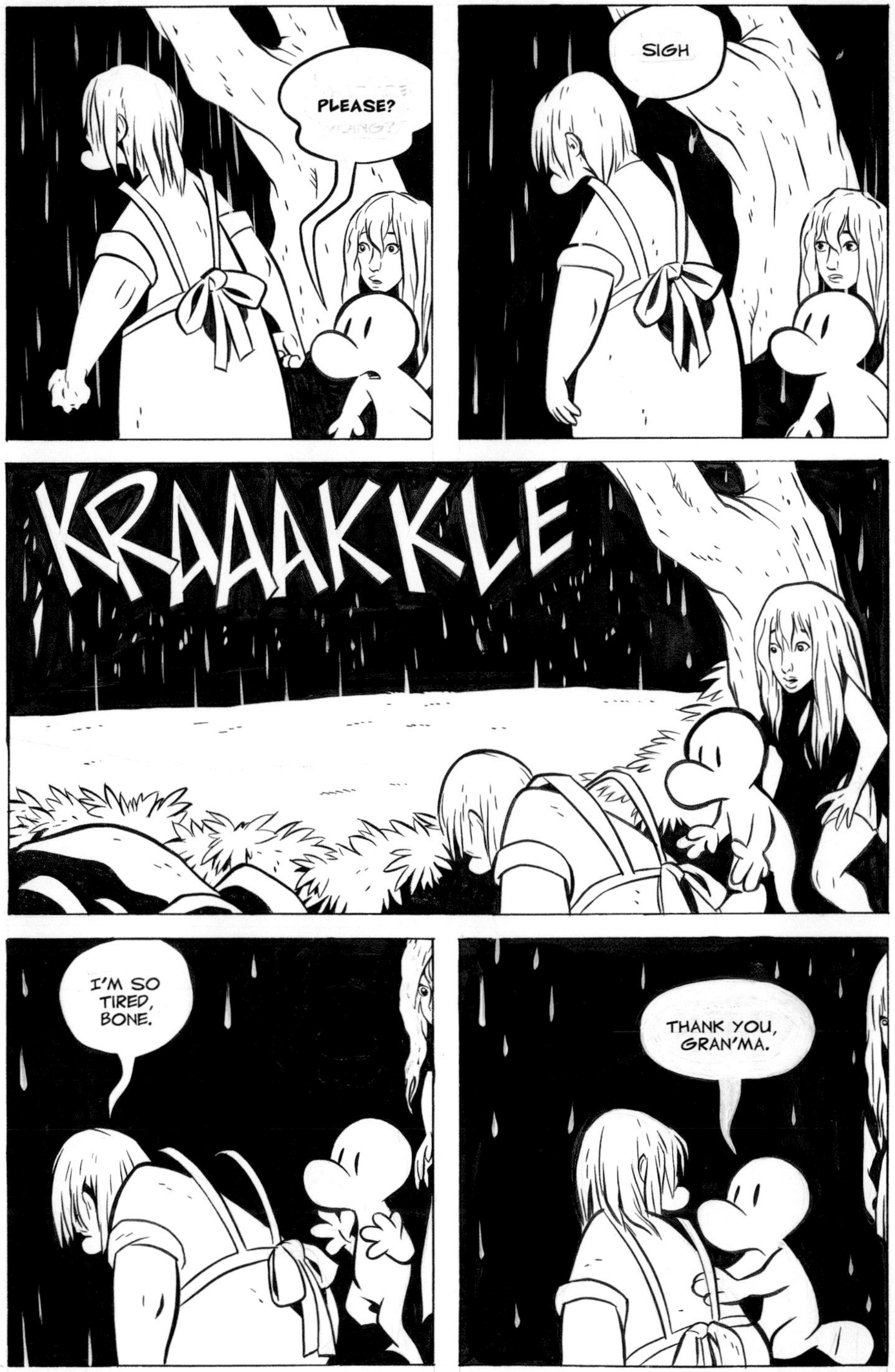
PLEASE?
SIGH
KRAAAKKLE
I'M SO TIRED, BONE.
THANK YOU, GRAN'MA.

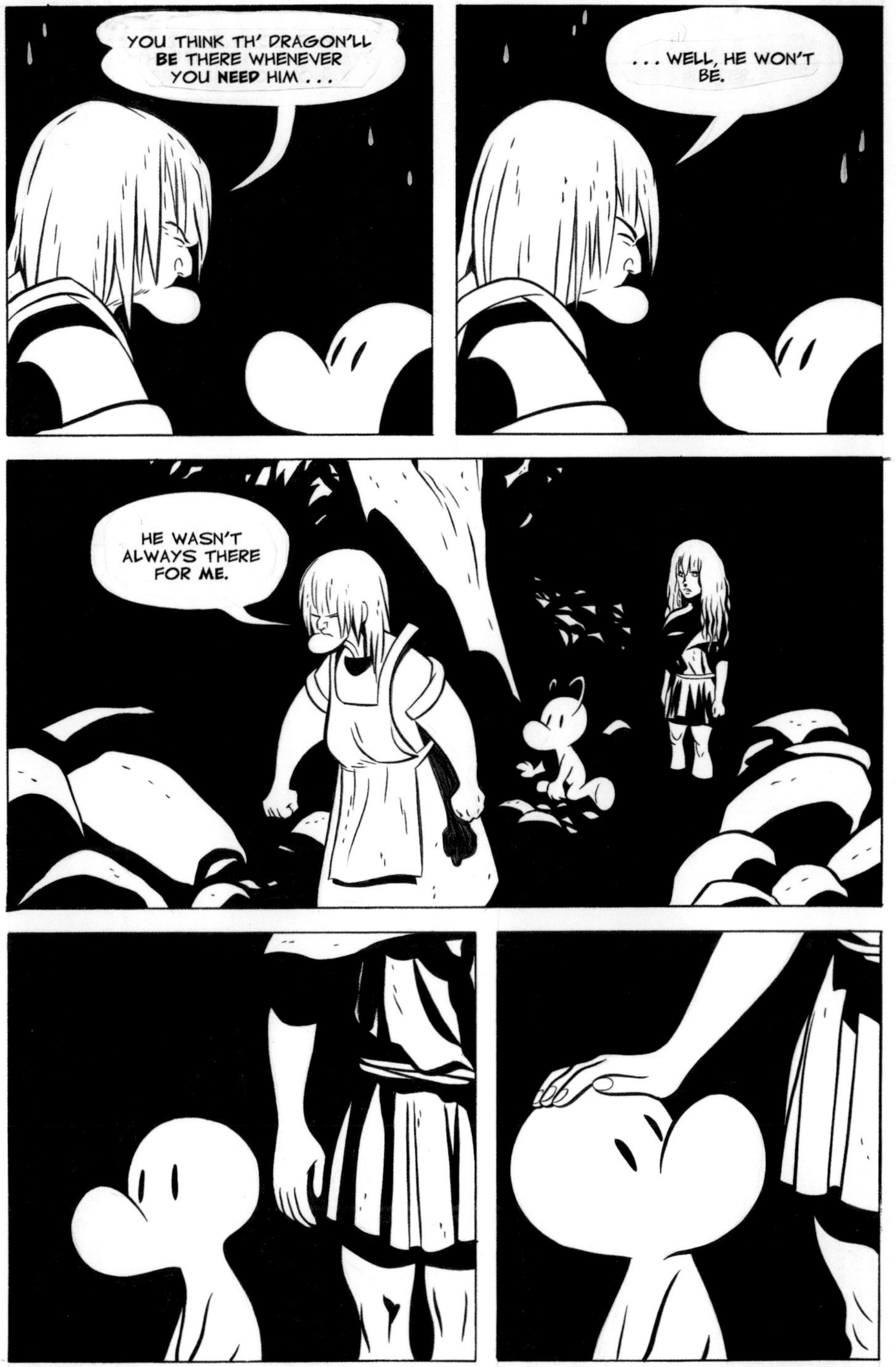
YOU THINK TH' DRAGON'LL BE THERE WHENEVER YOU NEED HIM . . .
. . . WELL, HE WON'T BE.
HE WASN'T ALWAYS THERE FOR ME.

LET'S GO HOME.
AND WHEN WE GET THERE, TRY TO FIND YOUR KNAPSACK, OKAY?
I THINK IT'S TIME WE SHOWED GRAN'MA OUR MAP.

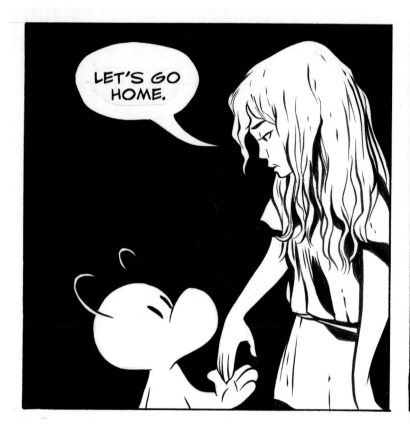

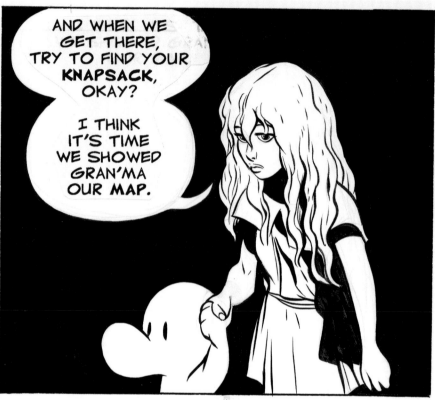

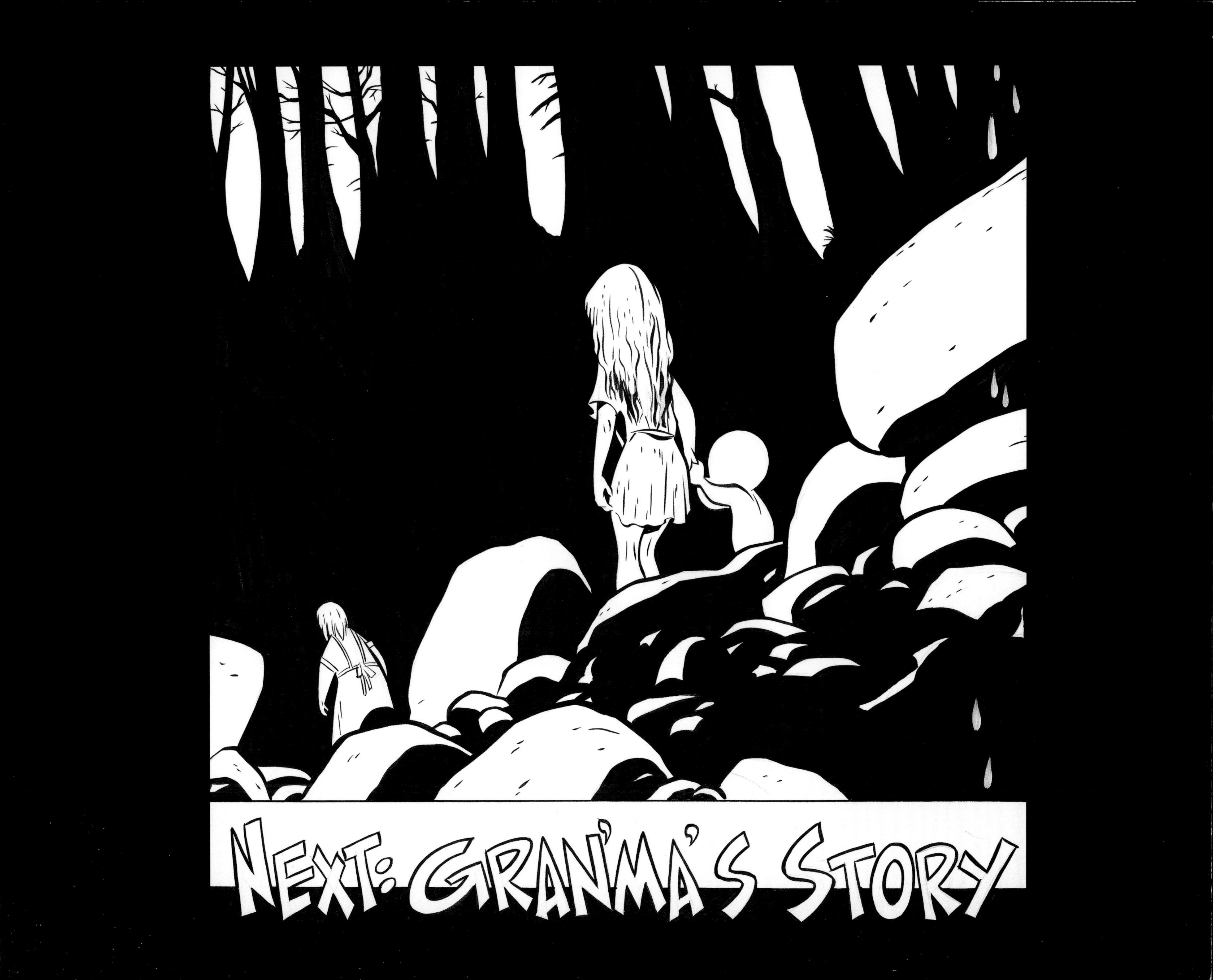
NEXT: GRAN'MA'S STORY

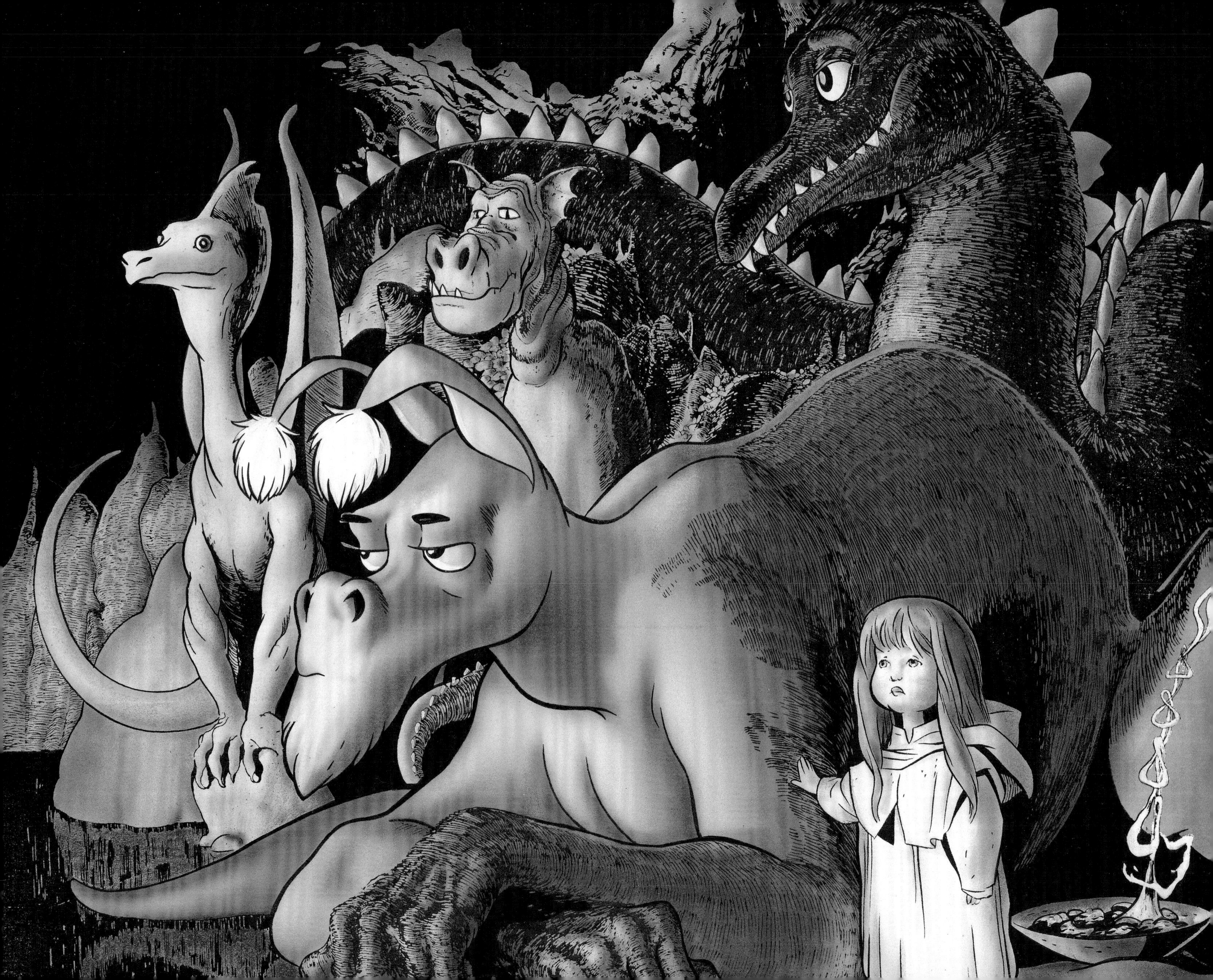

# Bone Notes

Neil Gaiman

I was reading *Bone* from almost the beginning, having been handed the first two comics by Mark Askwith after a signing in Toronto. "You'll like these," he said. I bought *Bone* until I met Jeff Smith, and he started sending it to me and I stopped buying it, but month in and month out, I read it as the years went by, until at last it was done.

I even wrote an introduction to the second volume of *Bone, The Great Cow Race*. (Which, because the edition with the introduction has been out of print for over a decade now, and you probably haven't read it, and if you have, you've forgotten it, I shall now proceed to reprint here.)

> Readers tend to have two reactions to Herman Melville's remarkable novel, *Moby-Dick or The Whale.*
>
> Either they respond to the seafaring adventure yarn, with its huge, gaping, obsessive travelogue, but they hurry through Melville's chapters with titles like "The Sperm Whale's Head—Contrasted View"; or they find themselves becoming obsessed with Melville's retelling of the minutiae of whaling and the Physiognomy of Whales, and with all the strange, experimental layers of creaking, wind-lashed, bloody-handed life aboard the Pequod, but becoming almost impatient with the tale of Ahab and Moby Dick (and why *Moby-Dick* is hyphenated when it's the title of the book and not when it's the name of the whale is a mystery that passeth all understanding).
>
> The first time I read *Moby-Dick*, as a boy of ten, I read it for the exciting bits (and finished it convinced that it would make a terrific comic; then again, I recall, at about the same age, finishing *King Solomon's Mines* utterly certain that it would make a brilliant musical. I must, in retrospect, have been an odd child). More recently, as an elderly gentleman of three-and-thirty, sent back to *Moby-Dick* by the urgings of Jeff Smith and a long plane flight or two, I discovered that I was enjoying the thing as a whole, with the broken spars of previous drafts sticking out of its side.
>
> Which is analogous in some ways to the experience of reading *Bone*. When I first read the stories here assembled, the parts I prized were the glittering set-pieces: the stupid, stupid rat-creatures, the honey hunt, the Great Cow Race, Fone Bone's heart-breakingly heart-felt love poems. That stuff's the accessible level of *Bone*, the stuff one latches onto immediately. It took a second reading—significantly, it took reading the whole six issues in one

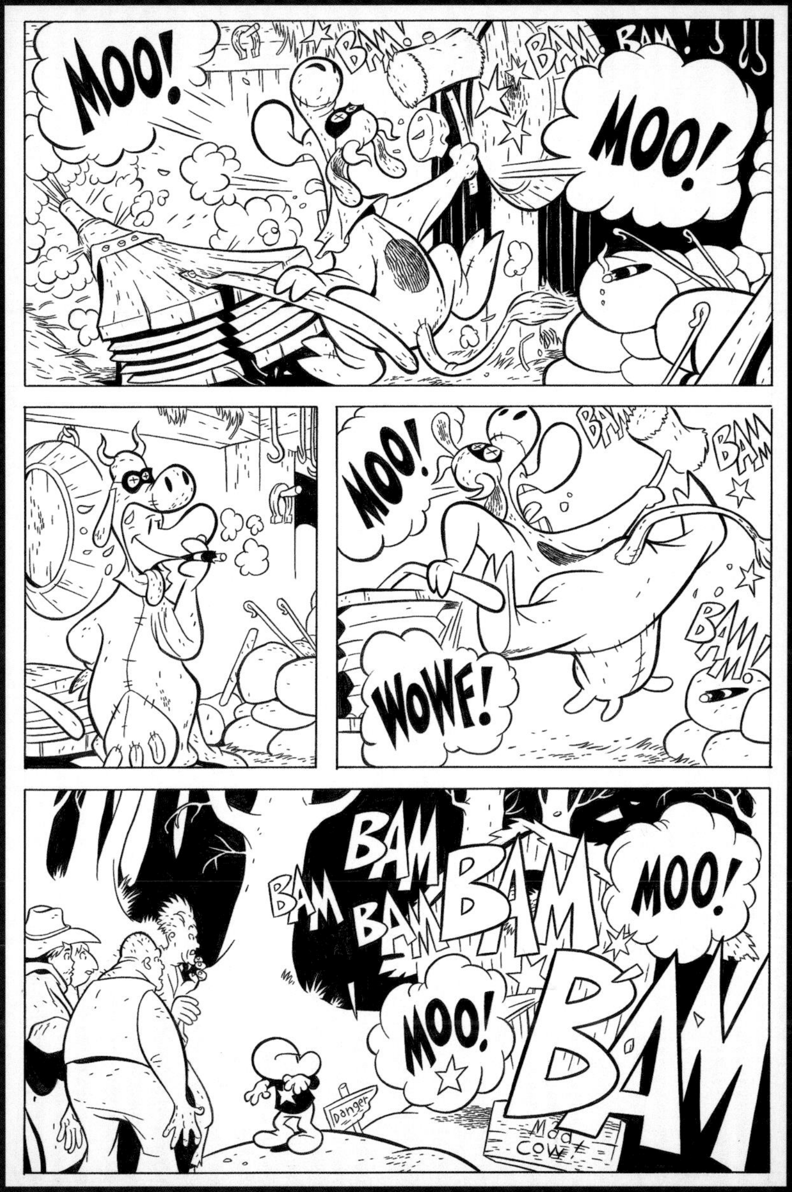

MOO!
BAM
BAM!
BAM!
MOO!
MOO!
BAM
BAM
WOWF!
BAM!
BAM
BAM
BAM
BAM
MOO!
MOO!
BAM
Danger
Mad Cow


*Bone* 8, cover, color (detail), 1993
Ink, airbrush, and colored pencils; airbrush by David Reed
17 x 14 in.

*Bone* 9, p. 17, 1993
(*Bone: The Complete Cartoon Epic in One Volume*, p. 211)
Ink and blue pencil on paper
17 x 14 in.

go—for me to appreciate the subtler back story, the delicate, dreamlike hints about Thorn's childhood, the sensation of huge forces massing on innocents.

The first long slurp of *Bone* has a certain aroma of Walt Kelly, and a bracing tang of Chuck Jones. It's the second sip that lingers, though. That's when you realize that there's more than that, a little Tolkien, a touch of Mallory, even a little smidgen of the Brothers Grimm…

I was introduced to *Bone* by Mark Askwith, who (and I place my life upon the line here for revealing one of the Big Secrets to the reading public) is one of the Secret People Behind Everything. He gave me the first few *Bones* when I was in Toronto being interviewed on the television show Mark produced, the late, lamented *Prisoners of Gravity*. I read them in an airport waiting room, and I laughed and winced, and admiration for its creator and publisher has only increased.

Jeff Smith can pace a joke better than almost anyone in comics (the only person who gives him a run for his money here is the brilliant Dave Sim); his dialogue is delightful, and I am in love with all his people, not to mention his animals, his villains, and even his bugs. This collection, the second, contains a number of individual moments you will enjoy (I say this without knowing you, perhaps presuming on our relationship a little, foreword-writer to potential reader, but I daresay I'm right nonetheless), and I repeat, it bears rereading.

The locale of *Bone* is that of the imagination. "It is not down on any map," as Melville said of the island of Kokovoko. "True places never are."

The world of *Bone* is a true place. And the map is only another part of the puzzle…

And with that, I pass you over to Jeff Smith. You are in capable hands. There is no one else I would trust to orchestrate a cow race; except, perhaps, Herman Melville, and his wouldn't have been anywhere near as funny.

There. That was what I thought when I wrote that, fourteen years ago. I'm happy to say that there's nothing in there that, with the benefit of hindsight, I'd want to retract or amend.

Still, as the comic went on, I began to miss the earlier issues—in Woody Allen's phrase, "the early funny stuff." I missed the *shtick*, the perfectly paced jokes. The cow race. The slapstick. I wasn't convinced that the adventure comic that *Bone* seemed to have transmuted into was enough of a replacement.

Rereading *Bone* now that it's all over and collected and in one place, I am struck chiefly by how wrong I was while I was reading it, and how very right Jeff Smith was, and how it was always, unquestionably, one thing, albeit one thing with tension—and a tension that, I suspect, helped make *Bone* what it was.

The economic model of making long comics stories is one that is based on the theory that the creator will need to eat while writing and drawing a page (perhaps) a day. So the food and roof are provided either by a healthy advance from a publisher (for longer works) or, more often, in a regular paycheck, by publishing a story in installments. So the normal model—the one on which *Bone* was built—is to publish a comic of around twenty pages every month or so. These comics are then collected together and published in book-length collections every year or thereabouts, and thus food happens, and a roof, and, in the case of successful comics, even clothing and shoes.

Thus the challenge for a writer or a writer-artist is to create something that works in installments, and also works as part of a whole. In a more-or-less-monthly story you need to recap information about a character last seen four years back, or about the sweep of a grand plot, or just to remind your readers what was going on in the story they read a month ago. (A lot can happen in your reader's life in a month.) You need to give your audience moments and sequences complete in themselves, resolutions that pay off, and most of all, you need to make it a sensible thing for the readers to have spent their dollars and cents on an installment of serial literature.

Dickens had similar problems.

But what you create as a monthly installment will eventually be read as a whole. A recap at the beginning of one episode might throw the timing of what you are doing off completely. The rhythms of the entire story—in the case of *Bone*, a story covering more than a thousand pages—and the rhythms of the collected part of the story and the rhythms of a monthly comic have different demands and different needs.

This is most obvious in the collected *Bone* in the first couple of chapters, when the Walt Kelly influence is at its height, and when Jeff Smith most needed to make the work accessible and bring people on board, and occasionally the pacing feels more like a newspaper Sunday page than an ongoing comic. The story is, or seems to be, in second place.

As a periodical reader, reading the book an installment at a time, when the story darkened I missed the tone of the first few years. I missed the Jeff Smith who could "pace a joke better than almost anyone," because the jokes were getting fewer and further between. I suspected that the nature of the comic had changed, and I worried that the lurch from Walt Kelly and Carl Barks to something closer to Tolkien had unbalanced the whole thing.

As I say, I was wrong, and deep down I knew it, but it was not until I reread the whole of *Bone* that I understood how wrong I had been.

The Bones themselves are an anomaly. They stumble into the story much as Unca Scrooge, Donald, and his three nephews might have crossed a mountain range and found themselves in a fantastic world. They are anachronistic, apparently irrelevant to the world they have found themselves in—twentieth-century creatures in a world of the fantastic. And it's here, I suspect, that the narrative tension is created. In formal Carl Barks–style storytelling, creatures like the Bone family inhabit a world like ours and wander from our world into another, more primitive world. They find a desert crossing, a mist-shrouded valley, an almost impassible mountain range—the things that keep us from Oz or the Lost World. They adventure, change things for the better, then cross the barrier to return to their own world.

Here, though, the world they enter is more complex than they—or we—initially perceive it to be. Characters who seem to be introduced for simple comedic effect have huge backstories, until the whole of the *Bone* tale begins to feel like the tip of an iceberg, or the end of something huge. The joy of *Bone* is that Jeff Smith knows more than we do. The events of *Bone* are driven by what has gone before. Lucius the amusing elderly innkeeper has a history with Gran'ma Ben. Gran'ma Ben is also Queen Rose. The Hooded One is her sister Briar. The love triangle between Briar and Lucius and Rose is one of the engines of plot. Still, even their plot seems like a postscript to the tale of the Locust spirit and the Dragons, as if the plot is a sequence of Russian nesting dolls, each of which is paradoxically larger than the one in which it was hidden. Each of the human characters changes hugely, both in our perception of them and in the way that they come to terms with their past and complete their already-begun stories.

The Bone cousins barely change, no more than Barks's ducks are changed by their experiences. Phoney is a creature of greed whose plans will backfire; Smiley is always simple, good-hearted, easily led. Fone Bone undergoes tribulations, including a broken heart, and takes a fragment of the locust into his soul, but even he leaves the story more or less as he entered it. Deepened, but still. Lessons learned are easily forgotten. Were Jeff Smith to take the Bone boys and send them into another adventure, it would be perfectly legitimate under the genre rules to which they are subscribed, although it might have the effect of lessening the impact of the first story, of Bone and the Harvestars. The Bones are cartoon characters, something that we are reminded of in the color editions of *Bone*—they work best with flat color, as if they are extra-real. The shading that works so well on everything else seems to lessen them by forcing us to consider that characters who are looping brushstrokes are actually realistically drawn, in the same way that, say, Lucius is.

The Bones have served as a bridge between the ongoing comic and the huge overstory that fills the *Complete Bone*. They acted as comedic relief, as subplots, as "bits," providing instant accessibility for readers who may not realize the significance of something set up, literally, years before. But most of all, they gave us tension. They set the plot in motion (after all, without Phoney's balloon none of it might ever have happened), and they made us care about it and learn about it, incrementally, in a way that we could never have done if Jeff Smith had simply told us the story of Thorn. They solve the problem of the big story, and the problem of the issue-by-issue story.

I had always known, panel to panel, issue to issue, how good Jeff Smith was. There is a special delight, however, in realizing that over the long haul he proves himself a master.

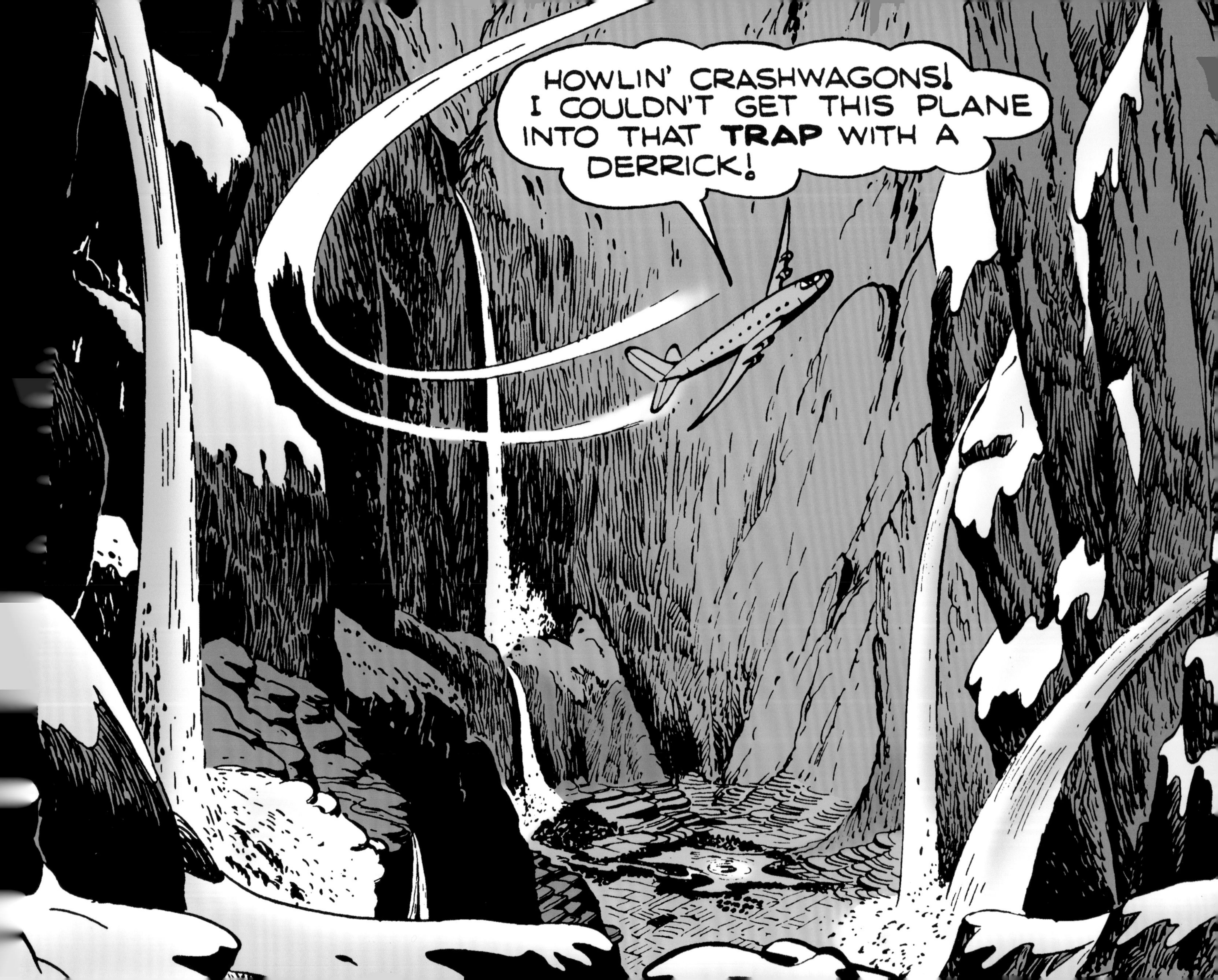
HOWLIN' CRASHWAGONS! I COULDN'T GET THIS PLANE INTO THAT **TRAP** WITH A DERRICK!

Many celebrated graphic novels are autobiographical or inspired by historical events (Alison Bechdel's *Fun Home*, Harvey Pekar's body of work, Art Spiegelman's *Maus*, Marjane Satrapi's *Persepolis* books, and Jason Lutes's *Berlin* all come to mind). *Bone* is unapologetic fantasy, the wonderfully original creation of author/artist Jeff Smith. Smith's well-crafted adventure following the Bone cousins—good-natured Fone, amoral and easily influenced Smiley, and greedy and conniving Phoney—kept me riveted for its epic, page-turning entirety. It also produced in me a completely unexpected Proustian sensation the moment I turned from page one to page two. The visually appealing Bone characters, their never-seen hometown of Boneville, and the journey precipitated by Phoney Bone's boundless greed immediately brought to mind a body of work that I devoured as a child: Carl Barks's *Uncle Scrooge* adventures. The connection is hardly revelatory. Smith cites Barks as an influence on par with Walt Kelly or Garry Trudeau, for instance, and others have noted the similarities in interviews with Smith. But the parallels have yet to be examined in any depth, and I believe a closer comparison of the two bodies of work is both appropriate and overdue.

Like Smith, Barks drew on early experience in animation.[1] His association with Disney and the company's characters began when he was hired as a storyman for animated shorts in 1936, but Barks disdained the collaborative nature of studio animation and left the company in 1942 to pursue a career in comic books.[2] He wrote and drew Walt Disney comics for Western Publishing from 1941 to 1966 and is best known for his work on the "Duck" comics, stories that featured Donald Duck, Donald's nephews Huey, Dewey, and Louie, and Donald's Uncle Scrooge, Barks's original creation. The stories appeared in issues of *Walt Disney Comics and Stories*, *Four Color*, and *Uncle Scrooge*, but because the names of the artists associated with Disney comics never appeared in the books, it was decades before readers knew the name of the person responsible for the stories that so clearly stood out from the others in any one issue. Barks's comics were the most popular in America for roughly fifteen years, but he received only average pay for a comics artist, and evidence suggests that Western Publishing withheld his fan mail to keep him oblivious to the size of his following.[3]

Carl Barks
"Tralla La," originally published in *Uncle Scrooge* 6, June 1954
© 2008 Walt Disney Enterprises, all rights reserved, used with permission

Carl Barks
*Uncle Scrooge* 13 (which includes "Land Beneath the Ground"), cover, March 1956
© 2008 Walt Disney Enterprises, all rights reserved, used with permission

Although Barks created shorter stories depicting Donald's relatively quotidian life in Duckburg, a representative "anytown U.S.A." populated by anthropomorphic ducks and other characters of less specific species, he is revered for the longer adventure stories found in issues of *Uncle Scrooge*. Those stories are engaging blends of comedy and fantasy with Uncle Scrooge, Donald, and the nephews traveling to strange lands occupied by exotic creatures and peoples.

A description of "Land of the Pygmy Indians," a typical *Uncle Scrooge* adventure story, may provide useful context for those unfamiliar with Barks's comics.[4] Scrooge's exasperation with the noise and smog of Duckburg (admittedly caused by his own industries) leads him to purchase a tract of virgin, supposedly uninhabited land north of Lake Superior. So as not to get lost, Scrooge brings Donald and the nephews along with him to scout the territory, promising them the chance to hunt and fish. This idyllic escape transforms quickly—to the nephews' horror—as Scrooge views the land only as a rich mine of exploitable natural resources. Complicating matters further, the land *is* inhabited by the Peeweegahs, a tribe of tiny Indians rendered in the potentially offensive caricatures common to the era. The Peeweegahs view the Ducks as intruders and are enraged that someone might believe in not only owning their land but also in exploiting its resources (a perspective vociferously shared by the nephews). The tribe offers the Ducks one chance to prove their good intentions: if Donald can catch a celebrated giant sturgeon, they will be viewed as friends. Donald tames the giant fish with the help of a makeshift noxious pill, created courtesy of the nephews and their "Junior Woodchucks" handbook. Uncle Scrooge surrenders the land, after smoking a peace pipe filled with more of the noxious elements, and returns to Duckburg, relieved to be surrounded once again by its pollution, at the story's end. The basic narrative elements here—a conflict over Scrooge's fortune, a journey to an exotic land, and an encounter with strange peoples—are quite typical for an *Uncle Scrooge* story.

SOON!
BROTHER! LOOK AT THE MILLIONS OF LAKES! CLEAN, BLUE LIKE SAPPHIRES!
I BET THERE'S FISH IN THOSE LAKES SO BIG THEY COULD SWALLOW A FISHERMAN!
MY LAND RUNS FROM THAT HOOK-SHAPED LAKE FIFTY MILES NORTH AND FORTY MILES WEST!
NOT A SMOKING FACTORY IN SIGHT! WHAT A CLEAN, WONDERFUL PLACE!
AND IT'S GOING TO STAY THAT WAY! ....HMM!... WHAT'S THAT RED STREAK IN THE SOIL DOWN THERE — IRON ORE ?
I'LL LAND ON THIS BIG LAKE! IT'S ABOUT THE MIDDLE OF MY HOLDINGS!
WE'LL EXPLORE AROUND HERE FOR A FEW DAYS, THEN FLY ON FARTHER NORTH!
THE PLANE SHOULD BE SAFE WHILE WE'RE GONE, SINCE YOU SAY THAT NOBODY LIVES HERE!
MY! MY! WHAT A SPARKLING HEALTHINESS TO THE AIR! I COULD BOTTLE IT, I BET, AND SELL IT IN DUCKBURG!

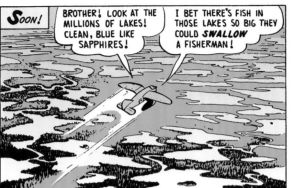

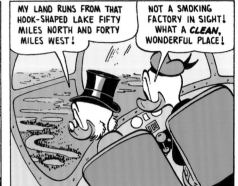

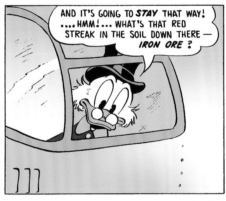

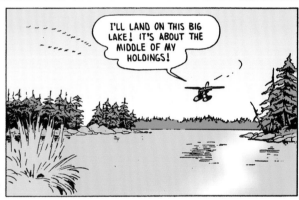

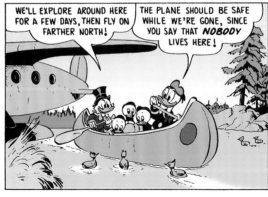

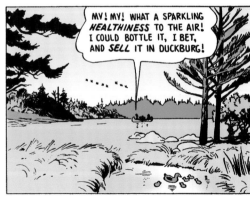

Both Smith and Barks embrace the fact that they are creating comic books—cartoony, humorous stories that, on the surface, appear to have no relation to the real world. (*Bone*, however, evolves into a darker, Tolkienesque epic unlike anything in Barks's Duck stories.) Their main characters are visually appealing in a traditional sense: round or curvy, cute, instantly recognizable, and accessible. By the time Barks began to draw Donald Duck, Donald was already an internationally recognizable character from the Disney animated cartoons. Barks could only refine his appearance, not drastically change it. The other major Duck characters—Uncle Scrooge, Huey, Dewey, and Louie—take the look of Donald as a starting point and are still among the most recognizable and popular cartoon characters ever put on page. In the contemporary comic book era, it is hard to find more original and visually appealing characters than Fone Bone (whom Smith once described to me as "Snoopy without the ears"), Phoney Bone, and Smiley Bone. All three are alluringly organic with rounded cartoon bodies and virtually no adornment other than Phoney's shirt and Smiley's ever-present bowler hat and vest. They are the types of characters that appeal to children and that endure.

This visual simplicity clearly contributes to the almost visceral pull of the characters experienced by readers of *all* ages. Barks's stories achieved unparalleled popularity despite the baggage of the then-prevalent notion that the comic book medium was appropriate only for children and barely literate adults. Smith, working in an era where that notion has (thankfully) been nearly extinguished, must certainly attribute the wild success of *Bone* in part to his adult readers. As of late 2007, the Scholastic color reprints of *Bone* have sold more than two million copies, an almost unheard-of figure for comic books. The Disney comics (which included work by artists other than Barks) reached their peak popularity in the early 1950s, when an estimated one in five Americans read Barks's stories, behind only *Time* and the *Saturday Evening Post* in magazine popularity.[5] Both comics have also attained significant international reputations: *Bone* has been translated into 16 languages as of late 2007, and Barks has been revered in Europe for decades.[6]

But the multigenerational and international appeal of *Bone* and the Duck stories can be attributed to far more than their visual attractiveness. Visually appealing characters might be enough to hold a young reader's attention for the length of an average comic book. More sophisticated readers demand fully realized characters situated in stories that are original and entertaining enough to satisfy adults. *Bone* and the Duck stories' success can be attributed to the fact that neither Smith nor Barks created stories and characters *for* children or that condescended to them in order to broaden their appeal. Here's what Barks had to say on the subject in 1972: "Kids are not empty-headed dolls, and they weren't thirty years ago. I can't recall a time when I was young enough to be ignorant of most worldly things. Nor did I ever know a kid who didn't know quite a lot about mechanics, geography, animals, values, morals, responsibility, etc. The vapid little Bobbies and Billies and Janies of the standard children's books are figments of the imaginations of old-maidish editors who long ago forgot what filled their minds when they were children."[7]

Smith is more definitive about intending *Bone* for adults: "I am definitely writing this for adults. The only reason it can be read by children is just because I'm staying true to the kind of comic I always wanted to read when I *was* a kid. And I still want to read it, but I'm an adult now, so I have to write it so I'll be interested in it! I was always looking for a comic with *Asterix/Uncle Scrooge*–type of characters with a more intense story, a bigger adventure that was more tightly woven and had more consequences."[8]

During his tenure working on both the animated films[9] and the comic books, Barks transformed Donald from a one-dimensional character with a hair-trigger temper to more of an everyman with real world concerns such as employment, financial security, relationships, and, in the *Uncle Scrooge* stories, acquiescence in helping his scheming uncle increase, protect, or regain his immeasurable fortune. The nephews, almost indistinguishable from one another, serve as a collective character that introduces both mischief and morality or—with their training as "Junior Woodchucks" and ever-ready handbook—an endlessly resourceful deus ex machina that often saves the Ducks when it appears all hope is lost.

Carl Barks
"Land of the Pygmy Indians," originally published in *Uncle Scrooge* 18, June 1957

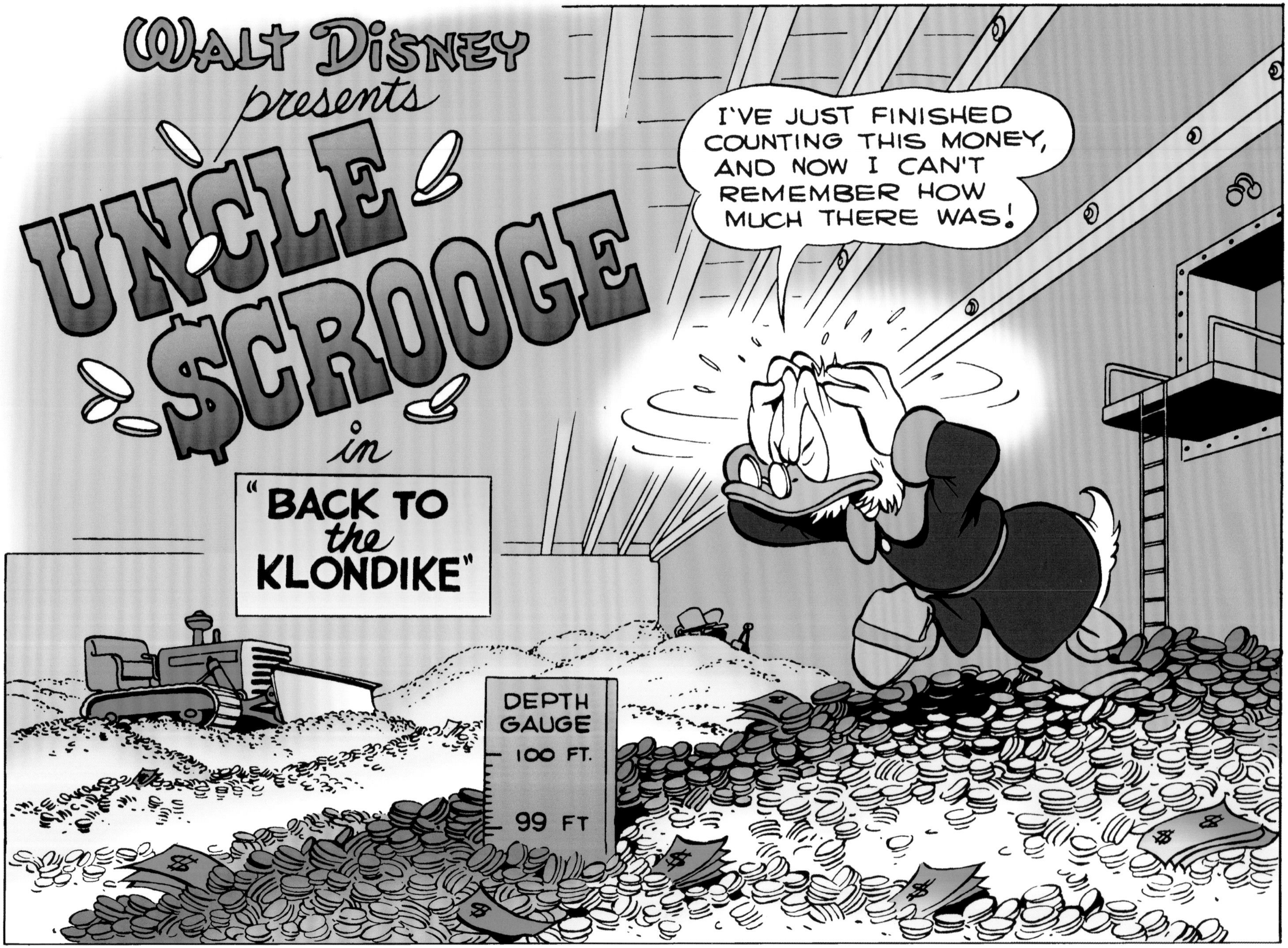
WALT DISNEY
presents
UNCLE $CROOGE
in
"BACK TO the KLONDIKE"
I'VE JUST FINISHED COUNTING THIS MONEY, AND NOW I CAN'T REMEMBER HOW MUCH THERE WAS!
DEPTH GAUGE
100 FT.
99 FT

Scrooge McDuck is a fascinating representation of an industrialist, in that his primary motivation in life is to *protect* his financial assets, often represented by a mammoth vault filled to the top with coinage and stray bills, instead of aggressively trying to increase his wealth. In fact, Barks contends that Scrooge is "the complete enemy of the capitalist system. He would destroy it in a year's time.... He would freeze under all of the stuff that keeps capitalism going.... Scrooge never spends anything, so everybody would get progressively poorer as he accumulated more of their money."[10] Yet, Barks has rendered him likable and sympathetic, and his greed is almost always reprimanded by Donald or the nephews at some point in each story. He is unwaveringly miserly and obsessed with his wealth, but Barks often provided him with moments of self-reflection and opportunities for redemption, as seen in the ending of "Back to the Klondike."[11]

In this story, Scrooge is struck by a sudden case of amnesia that causes him to repeatedly lose track as he counts his fortune and to forget where he placed the paper that recorded the amount from a previous tally. A doctor prescribes a medication that relieves his memory loss and has the added benefit of spurring him to remember a gold strike and an old flame, Glittering Goldie, from his youth during the Yukon gold rush. With very little exposition by Barks, Scrooge tells Donald and the nephews to pack for a trip to the Klondike. "Back to the Klondike" is the rare adventure that sheds light on Uncle Scrooge's past (much of the tale is told in flashback) and shows a softer side of the miser as he rigs a contest to allow Goldie to win the fortune for which he came.

From a purely narrative standpoint, Scrooge McDuck's greed as impetus for the Ducks' adventures is an amusingly familiar element of Barks's formula that, for me, is the root of the similarities I perceive with Smith's *Bone*. The Ducks' travels are almost invariably motivated by one of Uncle Scrooge's schemes, just as *Bone* begins when the cousins are expelled from Boneville following one of Phoney's botched plans. Throughout *Bone*, Phoney's greed either jeopardizes the cousins' safety or threatens to bring the wrath of the valley's inhabitants upon them, as shown in Phoney's attempt to fix the cow race or through his single-minded obsession with a return to Boneville with a chest filled with gold.

Deepening the similarity is the dichotomy between Phoney's and Scrooge's materialistic motivations and the practical ambivalence toward money displayed by all the other characters. In *Bone*, for example, money means nothing to the people in the valley who use eggs as currency. In the *Uncle Scrooge* stories, the exotic peoples encountered by the Ducks often don't value formal currency or lack materialist or capitalist impulses, which effectively situates them at odds with Scrooge.

THIRTEEN YEARS I SPENT COUNTING IT, AND THE TIME IS WASTED—JUST WASTED!
I WROTE THE TOTAL ON A SLIP OF PAPER, BUT I'VE FORGOTTEN WHERE I PUT THE SLIP!
MONEY BIN KEEP OUT
OR DID I WRITE IT DOWN? I'VE FORGOTTEN WHETHER I DID, OR I DIDN'T!
I'LL HAVE TO GET MY NEPHEW OVER HERE TO HELP ME COUNT IT AGAIN! I MAY NOT LIVE LONG ENOUGH TO FINISH THE JOB ALONE!
?

OPPOSITE AND RIGHT
Carl Barks
"Back to the Klondike," originally published in *Four Color* 456, March 1953

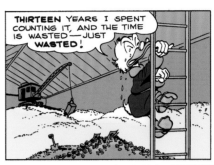

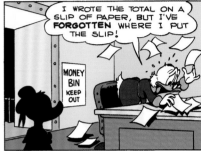

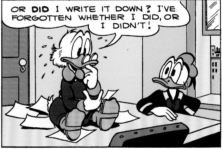

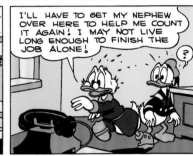

A pertinent example is found in "Land Beneath the Ground."[12] The story begins as Scrooge reads about a Chilean earthquake in the newspaper. Worried that a severe quake in Duckburg could cause his vault to crack and drain his fortune into the bowels of the Earth, he hires a crew to dig below the Earth's crust to search for any fissures that might threaten his vault. Once below, the crew hears mysterious voices and runs off the job in fear. With the work left undone, Scrooge pulls an I.O.U. from Donald (that, with interest, has grown from 50 cents to $500) to coerce him into finishing the job. Tunneling far below the surface, Donald, Uncle Scrooge, and the nephews discover a vast underground world inhabited by colorful, squat, bowling pin–shaped creatures, the Terries and the Fermies, whose main source of enjoyment is a game that happens to create collisions that cause earthquakes around the world. Like most of the exotic creatures and peoples encountered by the Ducks, they are completely self-sufficient and benevolent and only change when the Ducks intrude in their world. When, in hopes of ending the earthquakes, the Ducks steal the trophy that goes to the game's victor, the Terries and the Fermies decide to unleash the biggest earthquake ever. The quake cracks Scrooge's vault and his fortune empties into the tunnel. Thinking Scrooge is dumping worthless trash on them in exchange for the trophy, the Terries and Fermies return the vast sea of coins to the surface, plug the hole, and defiantly make Scrooge's top hat their new trophy.

More insight into Barks's views of capitalism can be gleaned from another story, "Tralla La."[13] Suddenly tired of the demands and controversies that accompany his wealth, Uncle Scrooge takes Donald and the boys in search of a mythical land, Tralla La, where money means nothing. The Ducks eventually make their way to the lost land at the base of the Himalayan mountains, following clues provided by the Junior Woodchuck handbook. Once there, Scrooge is delighted to be free of the burden of monetary wealth. Then Scrooge drops a stray bottle cap, and the Tralla Lallians instill it with the value of a precious gem. Suddenly he finds himself fielding offers for the riches of the kingdom in exchange for more bottle caps. A plan to fly in more bottle caps to make all of the inhabitants happy drastically backfires, as the devalued currency

MAYBE NOT! BUT I'M GETTING SUSPICIOUS OF THESE ROCKS!
OHO!....SOMETHING'S NOT RIGHT HERE! THIS ROCK IS WEARING A NECKTIE!
GET UP, THERE, AND GIVE AN ACCOUNT OF YOURSELF, YOU BALLED-UP HUMBUG!
HOWDY, PODNER! WELCOME TO TERRY FERMY!
GOOD NIGHT! WHAT SORT OF CREATURE ARE YOU?
A FERMY! SHUCKS, PODNER, YOU SHORE AIN'T BEEN AROUND!

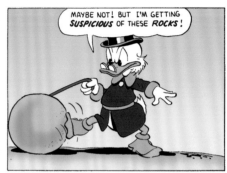

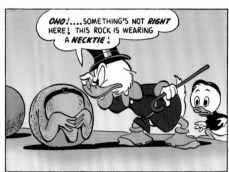

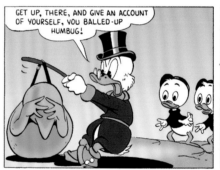

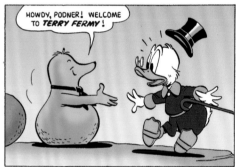

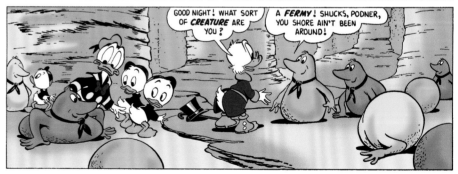

AT LAST I CAN RELAX WITHOUT HAVING A BUNCH OF PESTS TRYING TO CHISEL ME OUT OF MY MONEY!
LIFE IN TRALLA LA IS INDEED IDEAL— UNTIL ONE DAY—
HMM! WHAT IS THIS OBJECT?
IT IS THE SHINY STUFF CALLED METAL!... MUST BELONG TO THE OLD DUCK NAMED SCROOGE! I TAKE IT TO HIM!
I BRING YOU SOMETHING THAT YOU LOST!
HUH? WHY, THAT'S ONLY AN OLD BOTTLE CAP!

NOPE! THAT ISN'T WHAT HE DISAPPEARED INTO!
THE DRAGON!
WE'D CLEAN FORGOT ABOUT HIM!
I'M SURE THAT ISN'T HIM THAT'S YELLING FOR HELP!
HELP! HELP!


Carl Barks
"Land Beneath the Ground," originally published in *Uncle Scrooge* 13, March 1956


Carl Barks
"Tralla La," originally published in *Uncle Scrooge* 6, June 1954


Carl Barks
"The Golden Fleecing," originally published in *Uncle Scrooge* 12, December 1955


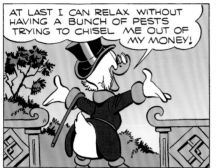

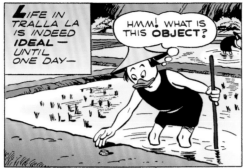

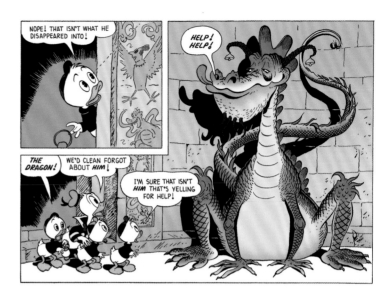

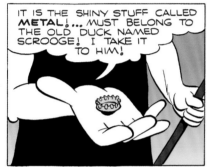

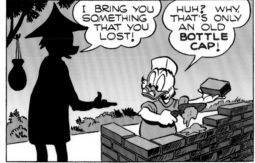

upends the economy and threatens to further destabilize the people's livelihood (the airplane drops of bottle caps destroy rice crops and grazing land). Scrooge promises to end the drops if the Tralla Lallians will let the Ducks leave. Once out, he is only too happy to return to the normal burdens of being a billionaire. Even the mere introduction of capitalism's residue (the bottle cap) can corrupt an otherwise innocent people.

Greed is one of the most unlikable personality traits an author can bestow on his or her characters, and in the case of both Uncle Scrooge and Phoney their obsessions with wealth serve only to make them neurotic, dissatisfied, and unhappy. The ambivalence displayed towards traditional money by the rest of the characters, however, softens the otherwise off-putting personalities of Scrooge and Phoney. Juxtaposing their greed with the attitudes of those with no monetary concerns (the villagers in *Bone*, the creatures in "Land Beneath the Ground") serves to make Scrooge and Phoney appear ridiculous by comparison and ultimately more sympathetic for their personal weakness.

I think the reason that *Bone* stirs my memories of a childhood spent reading comics—Jack Kirby's *Kamandi*, Joe Kubert's *Tarzan*, and Western's *Turok, Son of Stone* were among my favorites—is because it shares with them one of the most archetypal narrative structures: a hero's journey to and through a strange or "lost" world. This flexible storytelling device—the structure for tales as old and varied as Jason's quest for the Golden Fleece, Marco Polo's travels, *The Canterbury Tales*, and even *The Wizard of Oz*—allows the writer to place characters in an environment where rules can conveniently change to serve the story and where the characters meet new and exotic creatures at every turn.

In *Bone*, once the three cousins enter the valley, they meet a dragon, talking forest animals, a talking flea, fearsome (and bumbling) rat creatures, a powerful talking lion known as Roque Ja, and an array of human characters, whose degree of relative "realism" in appearance signals their identity as good or evil. The *Uncle Scrooge* stories take place in a long list of strange lands filled with even stranger creatures. "The Golden Fleecing," one of the best of Barks's stories, alone features dog-like creatures in Arab-style desert wear, a flock of vulture-like witches called the Larkies, and a giant dragon guarding the sought-after treasure of the story's title.[14] Both Smith and Barks ground their fantasy with doses of reality by establishing their characters within realistic environments.

AND LOOK AT THE *TIMBER* THAT COULD BE TURNED INTO *PAPER*!
YOU FORGET ABOUT *PAPER*, UNCA SCROOGE! YOU CAME UP HERE TO GET *AWAY* FROM PAPER AND PAPER MILLS AND SUCH THINGS!
THERE'S A *MOOSE*! GOLLY! ISN'T HE *TAME*?
MOOSE STEAKS SHOULD FETCH TWO DOLLARS A POUND IN THE NEW YORK MARKET!
*UNCA SCROOGE!*

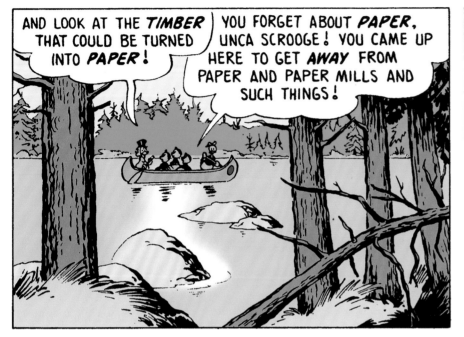

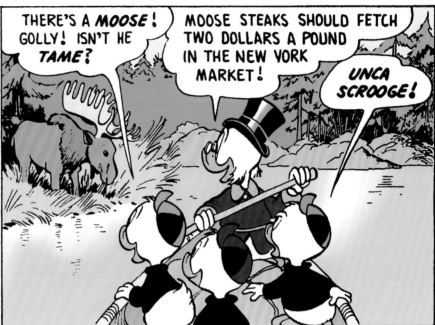

The forests and rocky formations throughout *Bone* are directly inspired by the Hocking Hills region of Ohio, southeast of Smith's home in Columbus, and the village of Atheia at the end of the epic is inspired by a trip Smith made to Kathmandu.[15] Similarly, Barks frequently set the Ducks' travels in real locations (Lake Superior, the Himalayas, the Klondike) and often renders these locales with a realistic precision that provides an interesting counterpoint to the very cartoonish characters.[16]

Comics art, like animated film, is a medium bound only by the imagination of the creator. An artist has the freedom to create any story, any character, and any action as long as he or she has the requisite skill to translate it from mind to page. While today's abundance of historical and autobiographical graphic novels has brought greater mainstream critical acceptance of the medium, there is something both refreshing and comforting about comics that celebrate the wonder and fantasy missing from many of these works. In opting for that kind of fantasy with *Bone*, Jeff Smith carries on the legacy of the great Carl Barks. Both have the rare ability to stoke that part of our imagination that is all-too-often neglected as we enter adulthood. In the contemporary comic book landscape, it is hard to find a more gifted visual artist than Smith, who has given us an epic story filled with humor, drama, memorable characters, and timeless themes. Comic book critic Douglas Wolk argues that we are currently experiencing the "golden age" of comic books with more diverse, sophisticated work being created than ever before.[17] True enough, and yet, amidst this wealth of great work, *Bone* stands out and occupies a special place reserved for work destined to be passed along from generation to generation.

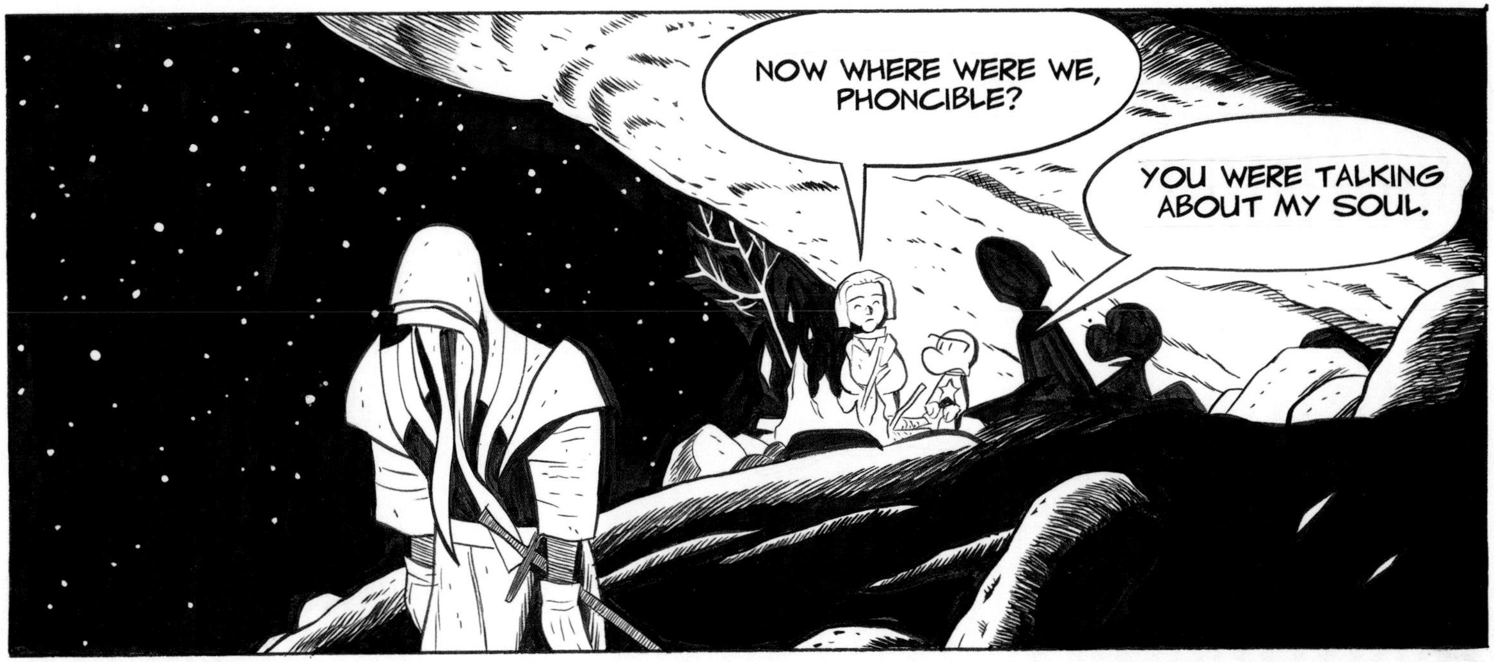
NOW WHERE WERE WE, PHONCIBLE?
YOU WERE TALKING ABOUT MY SOUL.

Carl Barks
"Land of the Pygmy Indians," originally published in *Uncle Scrooge* 18, June 1957


*Bone* 36, p. 15 (detail), 1999
(*Bone: The Complete Cartoon Epic in One Volume*, p. 801, detail)
Ink and blue pencil on paper
17 x 14 in.
The cave is modeled on Old Man's Cave, Hocking County, Ohio.

**Notes**

1. See Scott McCloud's essay in this catalogue for a thoughtful examination of the effect of Smith's experience as an animator on his comic book work.

2. Thomas Andrae, *Carl Barks and the Disney Comic Book* (Jackson: University Press of Mississippi, 2006), pp. 31–66. Andrae discusses Barks employment with Disney and examines the impact of his animation experience on his comic book work.

3. Andrae, *Carl Barks and the Disney Comic Book*, p. 98.

4. *Uncle Scrooge Adventures: The Barks/Rosa Collection—Volume 1* (Timonium, Maryland: Gemstone Publishing, July 2007), originally published in *Uncle Scrooge* #18, June 1957.

5. Andrae, *Carl Barks and the Disney Comic Book*, p. 6.

6. Don Rosa discusses Barks's European popularity in *The Comics Journal*, September 2000, pp. 51–53. Rosa is a comic book artist also celebrated for his stories featuring Disney characters, especially Uncle Scrooge.

7. Andrae, *Carl Barks and the Disney Comic Book*, p. 7; original interview by Paul Ciotti, September 28, 1972.

8. Gary Groth, "Jeff Smith Interview," *The Comics Journal*, December 1994, p. 86.

9. Andrae, *Carl Barks and the Disney Comic Book*, pp. 35–36.

10. Donald Ault, "I Never Followed the Rules Very Closely," interview with Carl Barks, *The Comics Journal*, September 2000, p. 64, transcribed from a video interview, c. 1975, released as *The Duck Man: An Interview with Carl Barks* (Prescott, Arizona: Bruce Hamilton Company, 1996).

11. *Carl Barks Greatest Duck Tales Stories—Volume 1* (Timonium, Maryland: Gemstone Publishing, 2006), originally published in *Four Color* #456, March 1953.

12. *Carl Barks Greatest Duck Tales Stories—Volume 1*, originally published in *Uncle Scrooge* #13, March 1956.

13. Andrae examines Barks's political beliefs (including his attitudes toward capitalism) throughout *Carl Barks and the Disney Comic Book*. "Tralla La" is reprinted in *Carl Barks Greatest Duck Tales Stories—Volume 2* (Timonium, Maryland: Gemstone Publishing, 2006), originally published in *Uncle Scrooge* #6, June 1954. Some stories were not originally titled and were only assigned titles in reprint.

14. *Carl Barks Greatest Duck Tales Stories—Volume 2*, originally published in *Uncle Scrooge* #12, December 1955.

15. Jeff Smith, *The Art of Bone* (Milwaukie, Oregon: Dark Horse Publishing, 2007), pp. 156–57.

16. Scott McCloud argues the effect allows readers to "mask themselves in a character and safely enter a sensually stimulating world." See Scott McCloud, *Understanding Comics: The Invisible Art* (Northampton, Massachusetts: Kitchen Sink Press, 1993), p. 43.

17. Douglas Wolk, *Reading Comics: How Graphic Novels Work and What They Mean* (Cambridge, Massachusetts: Da Capo Press, 2007), p. 10.

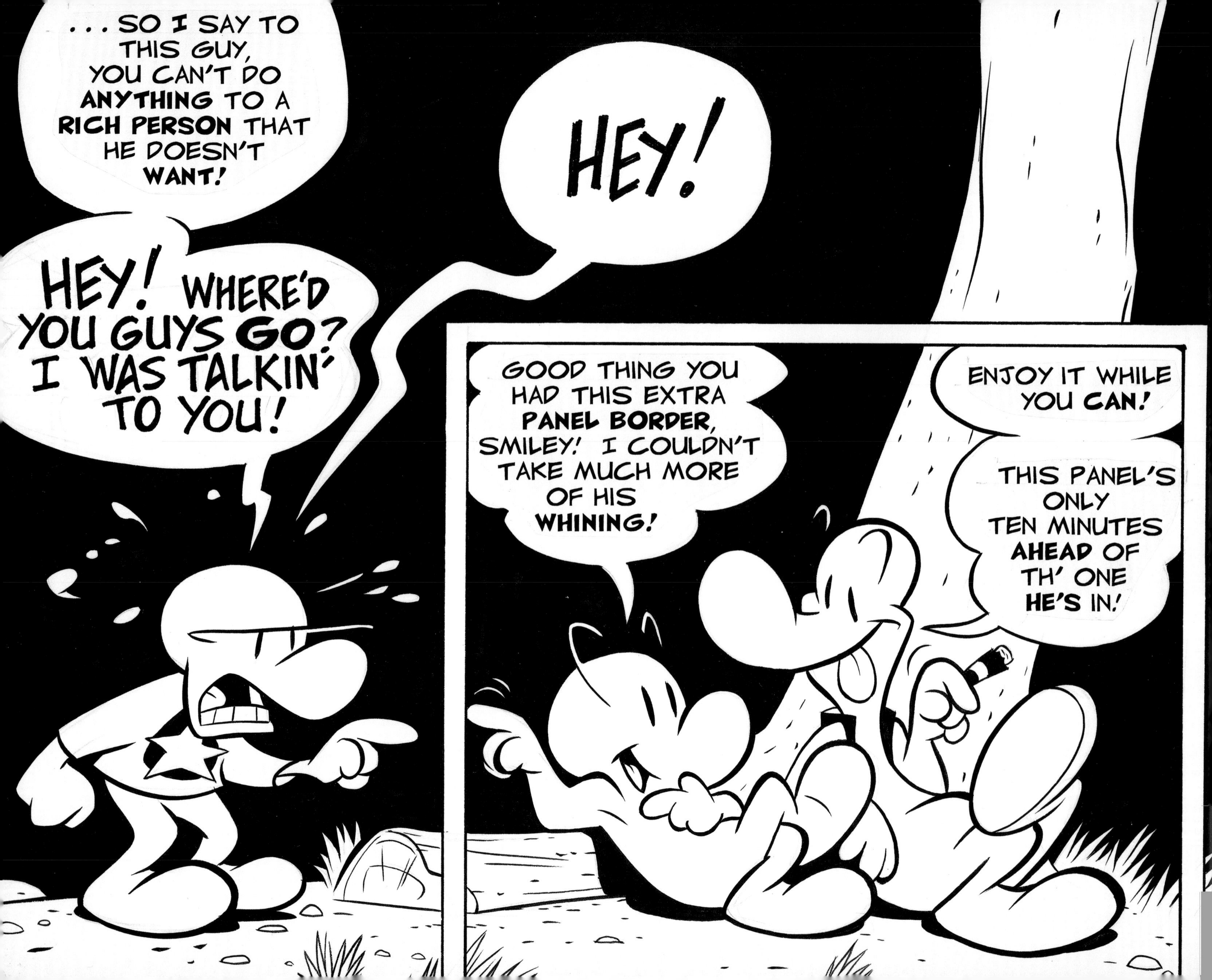
...SO I SAY TO THIS GUY, YOU CAN'T DO ANYTHING TO A RICH PERSON THAT HE DOESN'T WANT!
HEY! WHERE'D YOU GUYS GO? I WAS TALKIN' TO YOU!
HEY!
GOOD THING YOU HAD THIS EXTRA PANEL BORDER, SMILEY! I COULDN'T TAKE MUCH MORE OF HIS WHINING!
ENJOY IT WHILE YOU CAN!
THIS PANEL'S ONLY TEN MINUTES AHEAD OF TH' ONE HE'S IN!

# Jeff Smith's *Bone*: A Personal Appreciation

Scott McCloud

Stories, like their authors, are born to specific places and specific times. A discerning eye can place most stories among their cultural contemporaries as confidently as Londoners place each other by their accents, guided by clues that range from broad themes to specialized techniques. When a work of narrative art, or any art for that matter, earns the label "timeless" it's not because its origins have been obscured or rendered irrelevant in the quest for excellence—Bach's music belongs to the baroque period no more and no less than the offerings of a thousand weaker talents—but simply because it deserves to *outlive* those origins. In recent years, as Jeff Smith's *Bone* approached completion, his peers have gradually realized that while Smith may have been born to a specific place and time, he's crafted a work of comics storytelling that's likely to outlive him by a wide margin.

I belong to Jeff Smith's time and place. We were born just months apart, and although my first comics saw print seven years before *Bone*, comics historians will rightfully lump our early comics together in that relatively brief period—roughly the mid-1980s to the late 1990s—when comics stores in the "direct market" model were the only game in town for independent voices. From my front row seat as a contemporary, I hope to offer useful observations regarding Smith's place in shaping that period, and the ways in which that period may, in turn, have shaped Smith.

I also belong to Jeff Smith's profession. We've both spent the lion's share of our careers writing and drawing our own creations. Smith can add publisher and animator to his resume (I can't), and his command of the craft of drawing outstrips mine to a frankly embarrassing degree, so we're not peers in every respect. Still, from a practitioner's standpoint, I hope to also offer insights into the creative decisions made within his pages and panels, and the ways in which those decisions have contributed to *Bone*'s timeless appeal.

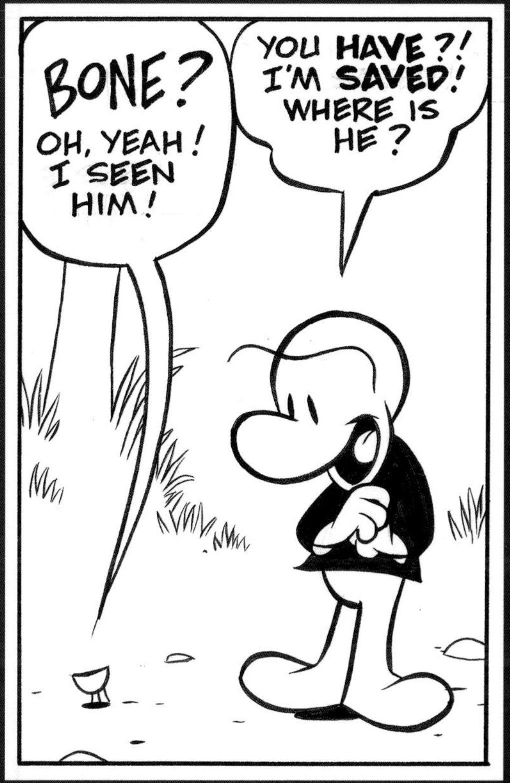
BONE? OH, YEAH! I SEEN HIM!
YOU HAVE?! I'M SAVED! WHERE IS HE?

*INKS: Cartoon and Comic Art Studios* 2, p. 1 (detail), 1995
Ink and blue pencil on paper
17 x 14 in.

*Bone* 3, p. 13, 1991
(*Bone: The Complete Cartoon Epic in One Volume*, p. 75)
Ink and blue pencil on paper
17 x 14 in.

## Time and Place

*Bone* first appeared in American comics stores in 1991, at a time when most North American comics artists saw themselves somewhere on a continuum from "mainstream comics" to "alternative/independent comics": the former associated with the superhero titles of Marvel and DC Comics favored by hardcore comics store patrons, the latter encompassing the efforts of virtually everyone else, from self-publishing entrepreneurs to creative visionaries to uncategorizable oddballs. Implicit in this dichotomy was a certain rebel flavor to the alternative and independent wing, stemming from the idea that alternative and independent titles were free to showcase more shocking adult content and themes. Many of them did just that, and some enjoyed modest success.

Less conspicuously, though, the alternative and independent wing also played incubator during this period to what advocates hopefully dubbed a "true mainstream" breed of comics: titles that might reach out to a general audience, including kids, and succeed far beyond the sweaty spandex crowd—if only that general audience could be made aware of their existence. Most failed to reach beyond the shops, because most shops failed to reach beyond their base clientele (a problem only partially solved as of this writing), but a few enjoyed opportunities to put the theory to the test. In *Bone*'s case, thanks to the patience and dedication of Smith and Vijaya Iyer—as well as a recurring spot in *Disney Adventures* magazine that placed the characters in every supermarket check-out aisle in America—the theory was well-tested and finally proven correct (*Bone*, in its current incarnation via Scholastic Books, has sold literally millions of copies).

Smith reached beyond the direct market commercially by reaching beyond it aesthetically. Rather than breathing the recirculated air of American comic book insiders, as many of our peers did, Smith opened the window for fresh ideas from animation, mainstream fantasy prose, international comics, and classic comic strips to rush in. Similar influences would inspire fellow travelers Linda Medley, Charles Vess, and Mark Crilley only a few years after *Bone*'s launch, and over a decade later, they still fill the sails of like-minded young creators such as those found in the *Flight* anthology. But at the time of its debut, *Bone* was virtually an anomaly.

Smith's work in animation prior to arriving on the comics scene was especially important to *Bone*'s popular appeal, its consistency of style, and Smith's work ethic. Traditional animation emphasizes the creation of lively, credible, internally constructed characters that must be drawn again and again in carefully studied poses and expressions with as little variation of style and shape as possible—skills tailor-made for good comics work, yet paradoxically lacking among the ranks of many of the field's professionals. While others took frequent artistic shortcuts—close-cropping to avoid drawing full figures, unnecessarily shifting "camera angles" to reduce the need for panel-to-panel consistency of detail, and fudged, imprecise linework—Smith cut few corners in his pursuit of the illusion of life. It's hard work to draw full figures in action from consistent angles with exacting details—even in the case of simply designed characters like the Bone cousins—but Smith seemed to relish the challenge.

Smith's comics career may have been hatched among the same rebel army of black and white alternative/independent comics creators that mine was, but he differed from us in one additional respect above all others. We were an egotistical lot who wanted to be celebrated for our unique artistic voices and innovative storytelling ideas. Smith's highest value—as unique, as innovative as he was and is to this day—was to simply tell his stories in as transparent, effective, and memorable a way as he could. No artist is without pride (art and humility have nothing to do with each other), but I'm confident that if a reader knew and loved the characters in *Bone*, while failing to even remember the name of the man who created them, Smith would consider it a fair trade.

## Pages and Panels

In *Bone*'s 1,332 pages, Smith frequently includes fixed-background set pieces designed to showcase the changing expressions and gestures of his characters. The rhythm and pacing of these scenes are pure vaudeville, but the compositions and visual execution are pure comics.

Sequential art includes all of the compositional tools associated with static visual art: shape, line quality, contrast, value, juxtaposition, etc. But, with the introduction of sequence, comics artists can also employ compositions of *change*, compositions of *expectation*, and compositions of *memory*.

In the page at right, the lack of camera movement or changes in background encourages us to look for small changes elsewhere. There is a figure/ground relationship between elements within each panel (quite literally, in this instance), but when taken in sequence, the "ground" can also include those elements that repeat from panel to panel, and the figurative elements include the parts that change—or resist expectations of change.

Panels two and three, for example, feature nearly identical illustrations, with three small differences. Our eyes are drawn to two of those differences immediately: the appearance of the heart and the fading of Thorn's smile. The heart is near the center and impossible to ignore (being the panel's primary subject), but the smile is small and subtle. If Smith had chosen a shifting camera angle or lathered the art with conspicuous, overly stylized rendering, we might have missed the smile, but here it's likely to be noticed by nearly all of his readers. Not as noticeable, however, is the quiet fading of the footsteps in the snow from panel two to panel three. It's a graphic decision to reduce clutter and brighten the area around the heart that we tend to pass over as we concentrate on our protagonists, and because of its marginal position.

HELLO.
UM... ARE YOU NEW AROUND HERE?
FONE BONE! WHAT'S YOURS?!
PLEASED TO MEET YOU, FONE BONE! MY NAME IS THORN!
THORN. THAT'S BEAUTIFUL! THOR--
THORN?! YOU'RE THORN? DO YOU KNOW A LITTLE BUG NAMED TED?!

*Bone* 2, p. 18, 1991 (*Bone: The Complete Cartoon Epic in One Volume*, p. 56) Ink and blue pencil on paper 17 x 14 in.

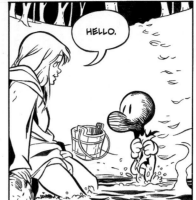

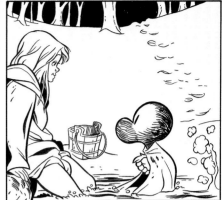

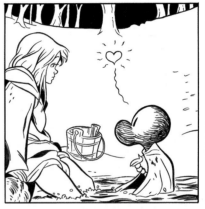

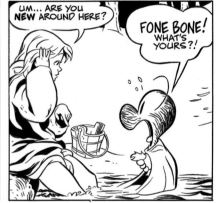

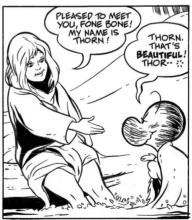

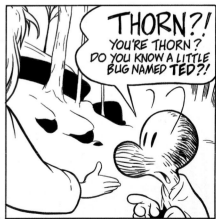

Our attention is also drawn to the *lack* of change in Fone Bone's position and attitude from panel two to panel three. Our expectation that Fone Bone will return Thorn's "Hello" renders the *lack* of same conspicuous. Smith knows that his tools as a storyteller include the knowledge and expectations of his audience—not just pen, brush, and paper—and that his readers are social creatures. Similarly, in the transition from panel three to panel four, our understanding of social conventions quickly identifies Thorn's slight gesture as socially appropriate and Fone Bone's outburst as being comically inappropriate—a contrast once more highlighted by the carefully controlled fixed background and angle. If we were to map those attention-commanding changes (or absences of change), panels one through four might look something like the image on the facing page.

The careful management of small changes in comics is nothing new. Comic strip artists including Garry Trudeau (an early influence on Smith) have long traded on the micromanagement of readers' eyeballs. But Smith broke new ground by inserting such tiny, childlike human moments into an epic adventure of almost Tolkien-like proportions; grounding his biggest events in convincing, human-scale terms.

Nearly all of the titles belonging to the alternative/independent comics scene of the 1990s—*Bone*'s spawning ground—appeared in black and white, but not all of their authors/artists embraced the format aesthetically. Many simply couldn't afford color, yet they still designed their artwork to accommodate it, in hopes that future successes could justify the expense of "colorizing" their work.

DOONESBURY
by Garry Trudeau
© 1978 G. B. Trudeau
UNIVERSAL PRESS SYNDICATE
WOULD YOU HOLD ON, PLEASE, MR. DUKE?
I'D BE HAPPY TO.
8-7
HEY, WHAT GIVES, BOSS? YOU ALREADY HAVE A JOB..
RILEY, MY BOY, IT'S A ONCE IN A LIFE-TIME OPENING. I'D BE A FOOL NOT TO AT LEAST GIVE IT A SHOT.
BUT WHAT ABOUT YOUR CONTRACT WITH THE 'SKINS? YOU'RE COMMIT-TED TO A..
FOR GOD'S SAKE, BOY, I'M ONLY PUTTING OUT FEELERS! I HAVEN'T SAID I'M QUITTING YET..
GBTrudeau
AND HE'S AN EXPERT ON DRUG ABUSE?
YES, SIR. HE SAYS IT'S HIS LIFE.
Rx

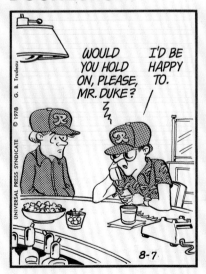

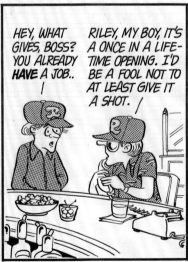

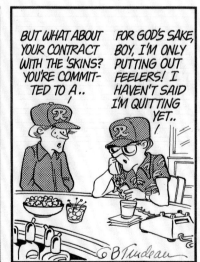

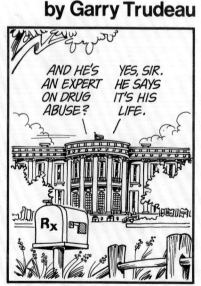

*Bone* 2, p. 18 (detail), 1991
(*Bone: The Complete Cartoon Epic in One Volume*, p. 56)
Ink and blue pencil on paper
17 x 14 in.

Garry Trudeau
*Doonesbury*, August 7, 1978
Ink, benday, blue pencil on paper
7¼ x 16⅝ in.

Such an approach rarely served stories well, however, since the line styles that had evolved throughout five decades of color printing on newsprint looked busy and over-exposed in black and white, with excessive feathering and haphazard spot-black placement. Few pleased the eye long enough to earn the color reprints their creators so desperately craved.

Other creators of the day embraced the unique challenges of black and white, however. The alternative scene had, since the 1980s, also played host to artists with strong graphic sensibilities who embraced the potential of black ink on white paper with enthusiasm, and that approach had also begun to mature. Artists such as Jaime Hernandez offered streamlined figures and faces with sweeping curves and perfectly balanced spot blacks and textures. Surrealist master Jim Woodring altered his style drastically when switching back and forth from color to black and white, emphasizing the unique potential and limitations of each in the process.

Smith is one of the few creators who successfully straddled the black-and-white/color divide in the model of the colorizers (another, earlier example came from Wendy and Richard Pini and their long-running *Elfquest*). The artwork in *Bone* appeared in black and white throughout its run but was eventually released in color editions, and both succeeded on their own terms. This was due, in part, to extensive digital remastering prior to color publication, but the primary ingredient was Smith's own linework and compositions: graphic and bold enough to be legible and anchored in black, expressive and open enough to benefit from the addition of color.

That said, there are pages in *Bone* that seem most at home in black and white and others that thirst for color. Throughout the masterful thunderstorm sequence (at right), the oscillation of black and white is so central to the progression of events that color can do little more than literally "fill in the blanks." Conversely, in the sequence on page 83, we see the kinds of busy linework and complex juxtapositions of overlapping subjects that color can help clarify and soften; it's a page simply waiting for the digital brush and paint bucket to "complete" it.

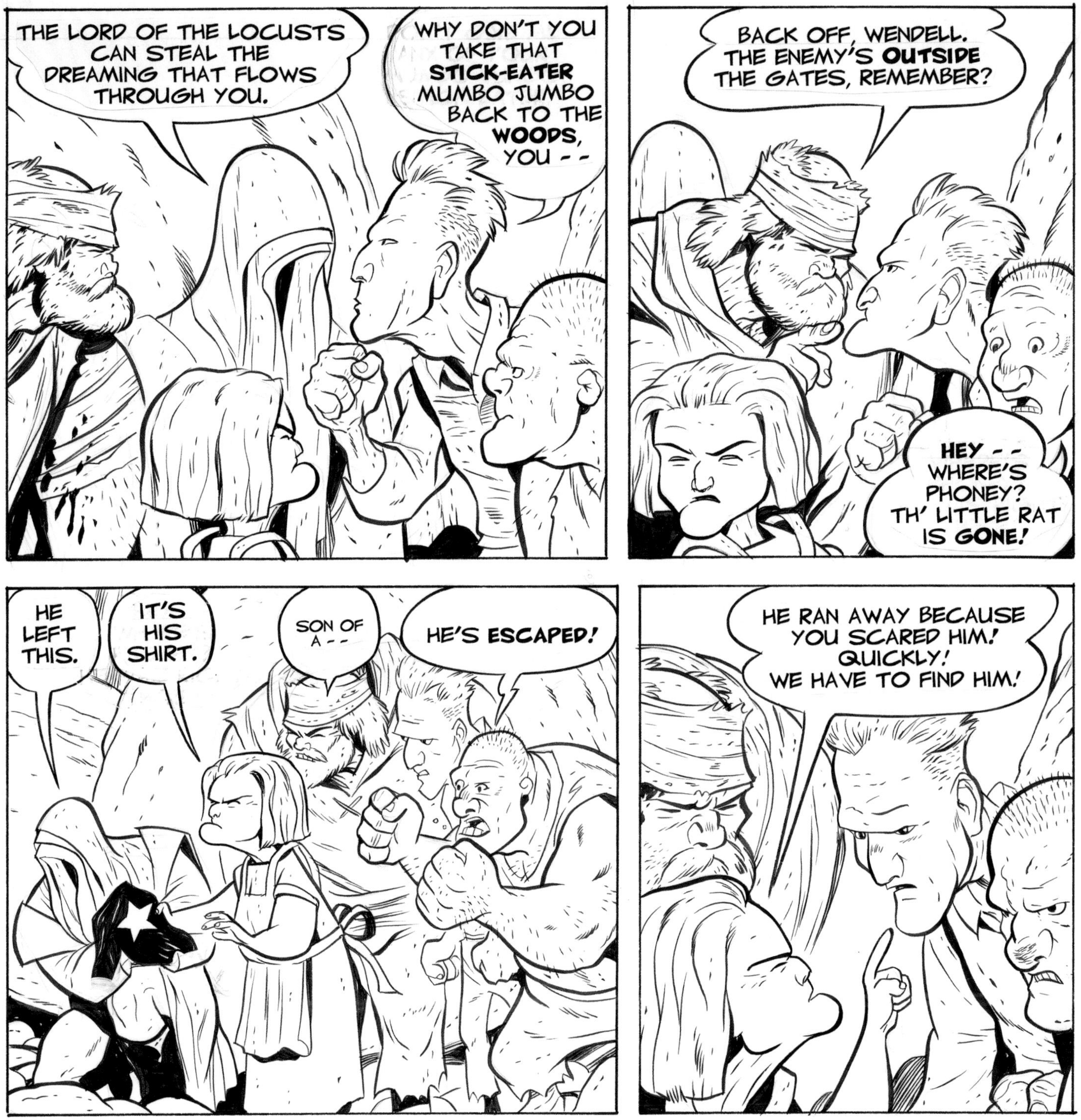
THE LORD OF THE LOCUSTS CAN STEAL THE DREAMING THAT FLOWS THROUGH YOU.
WHY DON'T YOU TAKE THAT **STICK-EATER** MUMBO JUMBO BACK TO THE **WOODS**, YOU --
BACK OFF, WENDELL. THE ENEMY'S **OUTSIDE** THE GATES, REMEMBER?
**HEY** -- WHERE'S PHONEY? TH' LITTLE RAT IS **GONE!**
HE LEFT THIS.
IT'S HIS SHIRT.
SON OF A --
HE'S **ESCAPED!**
HE RAN AWAY BECAUSE YOU SCARED HIM! QUICKLY! WE HAVE TO FIND HIM!

*Bone* 16, p. 14
(*Bone: The Complete Cartoon Epic in One Volume*, p. 366)
Ink and blue pencil on paper
17 x 14 in.

*Bone* 37, p. 4 (detail)
(*Bone: The Complete Cartoon Epic in One Volume*, p. 810, detail)
Ink and blue pencil on paper
17 x 14 in.

Perhaps the strongest ingredient in Smith's artwork, which helps anchor his pages in both black and white and color, is the design of the Bone cousins, whose Schulz-level simplicity and bold contours are as iconic as stop signs—and just as commanding to our attention. Many cartoonists have relied on equally simple designs for their protagonists, but Smith's approach is unusual because of the contrast between the Bones and their environment, as well as the contrast between the Bones and other characters in the story.

Smith's experience in animation may play a part in the former case. Character and background serve different functions from one another in animation and are rendered differently for reasons of expediency. A background can be used continuously for the duration of a scene with minimal changes, so it can be elaborately rendered. Characters, on the other hand, require up to twenty-four separate renditions in a single second of motion, so streamlining character designs can save hundreds of hours of work.

Beyond expediency, though, there are aesthetic reasons to approach character and environment with a different style or level of detail, reflecting their different functions within the story. In both animation and comics, the lines that describe the contours of a character's face or body are designed to bring that character to life and encourage some degree of reader identification and interior speculation. What are they thinking? What are they feeling? What are their intentions? On the other hand, the lines describing the surrounding landscape or inanimate objects are designed to evoke the *sensory* experience of those elements. Is it a warm day? Is the grass soft? Is the sword heavy?

When the simply drawn Bone cousins are juxtaposed with a more literal or elaborate rendering of their environments, Smith's art acknowledges that split function. We mentally "fill in" the simpler lines and role-play the emotions and intentions of the Bone cousins (even those we don't necessarily admire like Phoney Bone) and see/hear/feel/smell/taste the world they inhabit *through* their senses. We become them, and we experience their world from within, rather than as outside observers.

Such character/environment splits aren't uncommon. They can be seen in many Japanese comics and some traditional European comics in the post-Hergé tradition. More unusual, however, is Smith's rendering split *between* characters; specifically between the Bone cousins and their human companions. It would be a stretch to call human characters like Gran'ma Ben or Lucius Down "realistic." Their basic designs are cartoony and exaggerated. But compared to the Bone cousins, the story's human characters reflect proportions and textures far more recognizable from our real-world experience.

This split again reflects a split in our perceptions. As with the character-to-environment split, it encourages us to step into the Bone cousins' minds and see the outside world through their eyes, but this time that outside world includes those human characters. When Fone Bone stares at Thorn adoringly, we see her through his eyes far more than we see him through hers.

## Readers and Authors

It's been my privilege to watch a new generation raised on *Bone* begin to make their mark as comics writers and artists. I now realize, in retrospect, that my own generation took Jeff Smith for granted in many ways. We liked and respected his work, enjoyed his stories and admired his artwork, but I don't think we understood the full scale of what he was quietly accomplishing while we loudly sang the praises of the inventors and iconoclasts of comics' progressive wing.

Before a new generation could learn to love comics for its craft, for its inventions, or for its rough and honest expression, they first had to discover the simple joy of reading comics for its stories. Thanks to Jeff Smith, that discovery has been shared far and wide among more readers than we ever imagined.

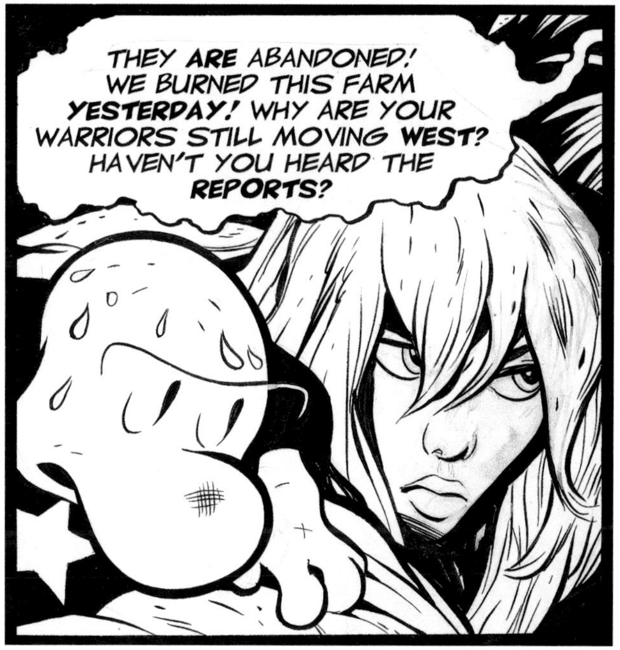
THEY ARE ABANDONED! WE BURNED THIS FARM YESTERDAY! WHY ARE YOUR WARRIORS STILL MOVING WEST? HAVEN'T YOU HEARD THE REPORTS?

*Bone* 49, p. 9 (detail), 2002
(*Bone: The Complete Cartoon Epic in One Volume*, p. 1095, detail)
Ink and blue pencil on paper
17 x 14 in.

*Bone* 33, p. 2 (detail), 1998
(*Bone: The Complete Cartoon Epic in One Volume*, p. 730, detail)
Ink and blue pencil on paper
17 x 14 in.

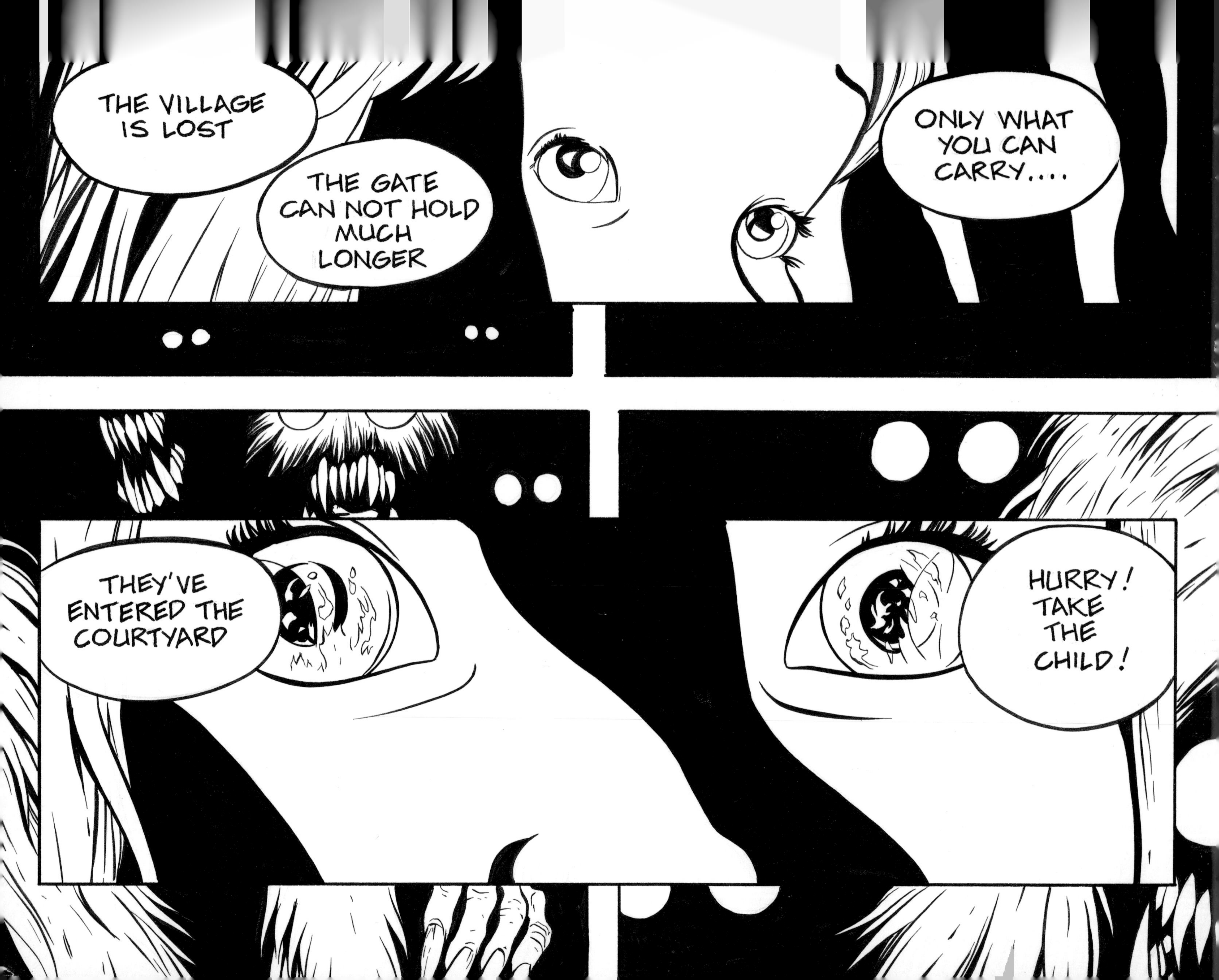
THE VILLAGE IS LOST
THE GATE CAN NOT HOLD MUCH LONGER
ONLY WHAT YOU CAN CARRY....
THEY'VE ENTERED THE COURTYARD
HURRY! TAKE THE CHILD!

# Acknowledgments

Jeff Smith and Vijaya Iyer clearly deserve the first expressions of thanks here, for their incredibly gracious cooperation with every stage of this publication and the exhibition it accompanies. We are also indebted to Kathleen Glosan and Steve Hamaker at Cartoon Books.

Scholastic has earned the gratitude of everyone associated with the project for its very generous financial support. Thanks as well to American Airlines / American Eagle and the Blackwell for their support of all the spring exhibitions at the Wexner Center.

Jeff Smith has kindly loaned drawings to the exhibition from his own collection in addition to all his other considerations, and he has our sincere appreciation in that regard. We also gratefully acknowledge Brian Walker and the International Museum of Cartoon Art for lending works from that collection and Stephen A. Geppi for the loan of a Carl Barks page from Geppi's Entertainment Museum.

Neal Gaiman and Scott McCloud, two of Jeff Smith's most respected and distinguished colleagues in the field of contemporary comics, have each contributed an eloquent, thoughtful, and lively essay to this catalogue. We're thrilled to have their thoughts and their voices represented here. For assistance with other aspects of the catalogue, we thank Katie Popoff, who transcribed the conversation that adds Jeff's own voice to the book, and John Clark at Gemstone Publishing, who aided us in obtaining illustrations of Carl Barks's images from the *Uncle Scrooge* books.

Our colleagues have been enormously supportive of *Bone and Beyond* without exception. At the Wexner Center, the list begins with Director Sherri Geldin, who gave us not only the go ahead for this untraditional show but her unswerving enthusiasm. Our core team from the exhibitions department has cordially shared its considerable expertise with the myriad responsibilities of mounting an exhibition, and we thank Manager of Exhibitions Jill Davis, Head Registrar Megan Cavanaugh, Preparator Will Fugman and the installation crew, and Curatorial Assistant Nancy Schindele. Bill Horrigan, Jennifer Lange, Chris Stults, Paul Hill, and Mike Olenick of the Wexner Center's media arts department and Jenny Robb, Susan Liberator, Marilyn Scott, Jillian Carney, and Colin McDonald at the Cartoon Research Library all have our gratitude for the assistance, understanding, and patience that made it possible for both of us to participate in this project. We send special thanks to Jenny Robb for her insight and expertise in support of many aspects of the catalogue and exhibition and to Chris Stults for his valuable counsel about all things related to comic books.

Numerous other colleagues at the Wexner Center have worked closely with us. Amanda Potter, Educator for Public and University Programs, aided in organizing an intriguing slate of lectures to complement the exhibition; Matt Reber, Manager of the Wexner Center Store, coordinated several accompanying book signings. Director of Design M. Christopher Jones and Editor Ann Bremner worked to realize a handsome exhibition catalogue that's well attuned to the sensibility of its contents. Director of Development Jeffrey Byars, Senior Development Officer Lisa Wente, Director of Marketing and Communications Jerry Dannemiller, Director of Media and Public Relations Karen Simonian, and many additional staff members from their respective areas, offered significant assistance as well. Thanks, in short, to the entire staff.

Finally, each of us thanks the other for a most rewarding co-conspiracy on *Jeff Smith: Bone and Beyond.* This collaboration has been collegial, productive, fun—and an excellent basis for ongoing cooperation.

Lucy Shelton Caswell
David Filipi

*Bone* 4, p. 21 (detail), 1992
(*Bone: The Complete Cartoon Epic in One Volume,* p. 105, detail)
Ink and blue pencil on paper
17 x 14 in.

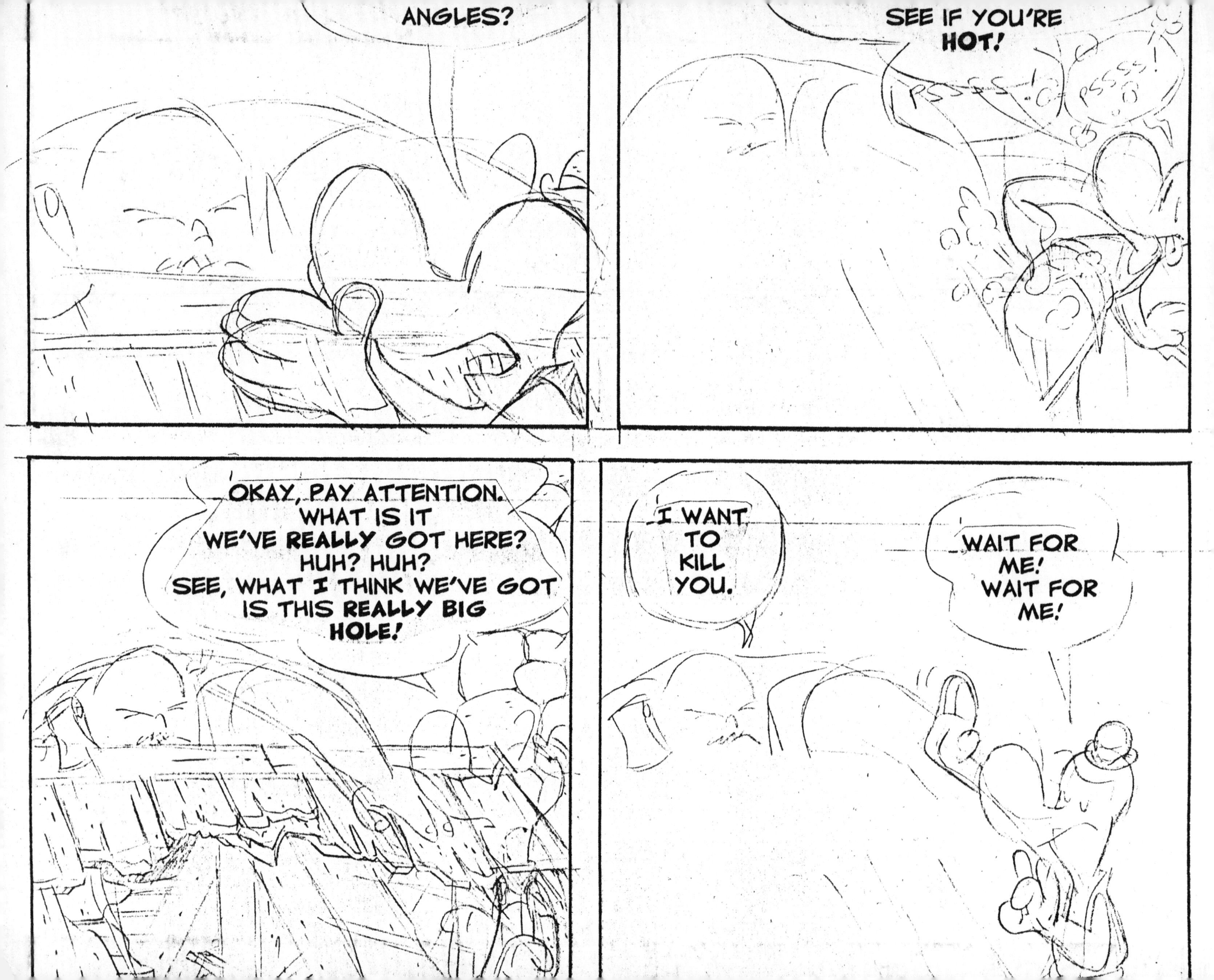
ANGLES?
SEE IF YOU'RE **HOT!**
OKAY, PAY ATTENTION. WHAT IS IT WE'VE **REALLY** GOT HERE? HUH? HUH? SEE, WHAT I THINK WE'VE GOT IS THIS **REALLY BIG HOLE!**
I WANT TO KILL YOU.
WAIT FOR ME! WAIT FOR ME!